HOOP SKIRTS
&
PONY TAILS

Jacky Hyams is a freelance journalist and non-fiction author who has written for a wide range of magazines and newspapers in the UK and Australia, including the *Sydney Morning Herald*, *Cosmopolitan*, *Rolling Stone*, the *Australian Women's Weekly* and the London *Evening Standard*.

She is the author of ten non-fiction books. These include two previous personal memoirs about post-war London, *Bombsites & Lollipops: My 1950s East End Childhood* and *White Boots & Miniskirts: A True Story about London in the Swinging Sixties*, published by John Blake Publishing.

Other bestselling recent books include *Bomb Girls: Britain's Secret Army* and *Frances Kray: The Tragic Bride*, the story of Reggie Kray's first wife, Frances Shea, also published by John Blake.

CONTENTS

ACKNOWLEDGEMENTS   ix

AUTHOR'S NOTE   xi

INTRODUCTION   1

CHAPTER 1 A SECRET: Hemsworth, Yorkshire, 1951   7

CHAPTER 2 THE ELEVEN-PLUS: Trafalgar Square,
     London, 4 July 1954   31

CHAPTER 3 THE WOMAN FROM CHATS   59

CHAPTER 4 SET ON THE CREST OF A BUSY HILL   87

CHAPTER 5 MESMERISED   117

CHAPTER 6 A CORSET   149

CHAPTER 7 END OF AN ERA   179

CHAPTER 8 NEW WORLDS   209

CHAPTER 9 THE 38 BUS TO FREEDOM   239

A FIFTIES MEMOIR

HOOP SKIRTS & PONY TAILS

JACKY HYAMS

JOHN BLAKE

Published by
John Blake Publishing Limited,
3 Bramber Court, 2 Bramber Road,
London W14 9PB, England

www.johnblakebooks.com

www.facebook.com/johnblakebooks ⑪
twitter.com/jblakebooks ⓔ

First published in paperback in 2016

ISBN: 978-1-78606-139-3

British Library Cataloguing-in-Publication Data:
A catalogue record for this book is available from the British Library.

Design by www.envydesign.co.uk

Printed in Great Britain by CPI Group (UK) Ltd

1 3 5 7 9 10 8 6 4 2

Papers used by John Blake Publishing are natural, recyclable products
made from wood grown in sustainable forests. The manufacturing processes
conform to the environmental regulations of the country of origin.

Every attempt has been made to contact the relevant copyright-holders,
but some were unobtainable. We would be grateful if the appropriate
people could contact us.

This book is for David Leigh.

ACKNOWLEDGEMENTS

Many thanks are due to my long-time friends who were happy to share their memories of those times.

Larraine de Napoli and Roberta Hart were generous with their time in remembering our teenage years. Eddie Knibbs's astonishingly vivid memory for detail was equally helpful.

Special thanks must also go to Julia Lipski in Sydney for her valuable insights into our family history as well as to Karen Steele, Mavis Hyams and Marilyn Manstoff for their recall of family history.

A big thank you too to the staff at Brighton's Jubilee Library, Hackney Archive, and Waterstones, Brighton: it's always a pleasure to deal with you.

Finally, all thanks to Toby Buchan at John Blake Publishing for his unflagging enthusiasm and encouragement for what proved to be a fascinating journey into the past.

AUTHOR'S NOTE:

PRE-DECIMAL STERLING

Decimal currency arrived in Britain in 1971. I have given prices in the old pre-decimal currency.

The pound was divided into 20 shillings (20/- or 20s), with 1 shilling made up of 12 pennies (12d), so £1 was made up of 240 pennies.

A guinea was worth 21 shillings or £1 and 1 shilling (£1 1s), and £1 was also sometimes referred to as 'a sovereign'. There were no 1-pound or 10-shilling (50p) coins, only notes.

To calculate today's value of any original price quoted, the National Archives has a very useful currency converter: https://www.nationalarchives.gov.uk/currency.

INTRODUCTION

Elvis was my first love. Things could only go downhill from there...

The arrival of the man with the swivel hips and the advent of rock 'n' roll might have seemed, at the time, to be the trigger for a spontaneous explosion of youth culture in the mid-1950s.

But the new music, the coffee bars with their shiny espresso machines, the juke boxes, the jiving, the teenage fashions that all seemed to spring up in Britain around that time were not quite a random, haphazard series of events, something that just happened out of the blue. There was more to it than that: certainly, teenage culture landed in Britain for the first time ever without much warning. But quite a lot of foresight and backroom planning had gone into it, too. The truth was: the marketing men had just discovered youth.

Catering specifically to young people, marketing to their tastes, their fashions, their fads was more or less unknown in this country, still struggling to get on its feet in the aftermath of wartime.

Yet when Elvis arrived, the undisputed power of the teenage market had already had a huge impact across the pond in the US.

The gurus of marketing and advertising, New York's Mad Men of Madison Avenue, had been quick off the mark. They'd already started to pick up on the huge untapped potential of the teenage consumer even before the American post-war baby-boomer generation was out of nappies. So it was inevitable, since so much of our culture, movies and music came from the US then, that the teenage market would land here too.

Wherever they came from, of course, the kids didn't care to dwell on the past. They cared only for a good time, to do what they wanted and to dress to impress each other, perfectly normal teenage behaviour.

However, here in Britain this was the first time in our entire history that the school leavers, the under-twenties, actually had the jobs and the money to pay for their good times. So it could never be a seamless transition. In many ways, the emergence of the British teenager created a rift between the austerity-bound wartime generation that had known mostly hardship and penny pinching in previous years, and their free-spending, jiving teenage offspring.

When I wrote *Bombsites & Lollipops*, my 'snapshot' of growing up in London's East End in the 1950s, the story spanned twenty years: from the end of the Second World War to the middle of the Sixties, an era which saw Britain emerging from a battered post-war world of grey skies and grey living into a more optimistic, forward-thinking era where anything seemed possible. Especially if you were young.

Much to my delight, readers of *Bombsites* wanted more, so I wrote its follow-up, *White Boots & Mini Skirts*, a personal perspective on London life from the mid- Sixties to the mid-Seventies, hugely eventful times that brought big social changes which would impact on everyone down the years.

But later on, I realised I had missed something important: covering those decades in *Bombsites* had not given me the scope to explore, in more detail, the central and, in some ways, most significant era of all: the Fifties. The time when modern Britain as we now think of it began to emerge and to move away from the shadows of the past.

This Fifties story is written from a personal perspective. Yet I became acutely aware, right from the moment I started to research and examine those ten years in more detail, that, in Britain at least, the collective vision of the that decade had turned into something quite odd, even unreal: the era had somehow been rebranded, as it were, as a far more genteel period, suffused with memories of a world unclouded by present-day hazards. A rosy, inherently safe world with kids happily playing in the street or pushing a bike over the cobbles, as in the Hovis advertisement, and family life reverting, post-war, to comfy warmth and stability. Not quite a land of plenty, of course, but a cosy, safe world of Austin 7s and *Mrs Dale's Diary* on the BBC Light Programme (now Radio 2).

Where did this rosy glow come from? The Fifties were far from comfortable. For many, the first half was harsh, an endlessly grey continuum of much of the previous era: more hardship, seemingly unending rationing, unkind winters, cruel shortages, political uncertainty.

Safety? It's relative. The air-raid warnings had stopped – but the general health and wellbeing of the nation, even with a brand-new free-at-the-point-of-use National Health Service, remained far less than satisfactory by today's standards.

Safe for kids? Certainly there was more cohesion than today in neighbourliness, shared endeavour, but what is often overlooked is that young people then were unlikely to rebel against parental disapproval or voice any disquiet about questionable adult behaviour, mainly thanks to the starched-shirt, tut-tutting, 'Be like Dad, keep Mum' outward respectability that had emerged in the war's wake. If there was a problem, you'd be better off keeping quiet about it.

Overall, the 1950s were repressive. Bad things happened to people then, just as they do now. All the same, the culture of ignorance or cover-up still reigned: that outward respectability concealed a very head-in-the-sand attitude – with the post-war authorities finding it much easier to obfuscate or deflect any criticism in a society still so determinedly class ridden.

The Fifties in Britain was largely a time of deference, where secrecy and shame for those that didn't or couldn't conform ruled the roost. Despite the heady promises of peacetime, everyone still 'knew their place'. Especially women.

Yet midway through the decade, in material terms, a shift came towards something vaguely resembling what we now know: the brand-new wonders of televisions, refrigerators, cars and credit, an economy finally on the move with jobs a-plenty and, especially for younger people, a sense of the wider world beyond.

For those like me, breaking free from formal education at the age of sixteen and stepping out into the working world, the promise of our future was exciting, exhilarating, despite what had been learned or absorbed from our families' experience of wartime. The repressive attitudes didn't vanish at the end of the Fifties. Even so, through the following decade, they slowly started to melt away.

Like most of my generation, I was a fairly innocent teenager. There was an undertow of the streetwise kid: I'd grown up knowing that my father and grandfather trod a very fine line between respectability and criminal behaviour in the way they earned their living.

I understood too that bribery – to call it by its real name – when they handed over cash to policemen so that they would keep quiet about illegal betting businesses – was a way of life in the East End environment we inhabited. Yet while I intensely disliked the grim physical environment around me, the bribery itself didn't trouble me – although the Fifties was, superficially, at least, a very moral era where families still attended their place of worship on Sundays in huge numbers and people still faced the hangman's noose for crimes that today might mean imprisonment for less than a decade.

This is my story, but it's also a baby-boomer yarn: Britain's lucky generation who were handed free education, free healthcare and, importantly, freedom from fear of unemployment, its background music the incredible sound of much of the greatest rock 'n' roll music ever created.

The Fifties had two distinct personalities.

In the first half, the nation struggled with a bad hangover from wartime, austerity and pursed-lip repression.

Then, midway, came the new consumerism – and the release into society of a youthful generation unhindered by the same fears or constraints of their parents.

Nothing was ever going to be quite the same again...

CHAPTER 1

A SECRET

HEMSWORTH,
YORKSHIRE, 1951

It was nearly June, but it was still chilly that morning as he slowly made his way down the creaky uncarpeted stairs and into the cluttered kitchen. He'd been waiting, hovering up in the bedroom until the minute he'd heard the door slam. He couldn't bear to sit, watching her as she picked up her shopping basket from its place by the side of the old wooden dresser, jammed the precious buff-coloured ration book inside her handbag and did up the big buttons on her shabby heavy woollen black coat, then carefully positioning her hat with a pin before making for the front door. Not this morning.

By now, there was scant dialogue between them anyway. He'd grown used to the cold, forbidding silence, her face set in a permanent sneer of contempt, the occasional plates of badly cooked food shoved in front of him, grudgingly, without comment. They'd stopped eating all meals together months ago. Her half-brother, her co-conspirator in what he'd realised, afterwards, was a plan they'd devised between them, had left the house, gone God knows where, weeks back. Thankfully. Something about a woman in Barnsley. Then she'd swiftly moved herself into the spare bedroom.

Once she'd left the tiny terraced two-up two-down in the narrow street, he knew she'd be picking her way along the Wakefield Road for at least an hour: time enough for her to queue for a few groceries, get to the butchers, grumbling as per the daily ritual with all the other shabbily clad, weary women, clutching her purse at the counter, carefully, grudgingly, counting out the coppers and silver, and bitching about the price of this, the shortage of that.

Six years now since war officially ended. Yet no let-up really, still relentless misery, the wonderful peace times they'd been promised so often nowhere in sight. Not for them, anyway.

Did she guess? he wondered. He'd been mulling it over enough these past weeks. Their next-door neighbour, widowed a decade back, perpetually addicted to Gracie Fields's voice, was indulging herself again this morning: the strains of 'Now Is the Hour/For Me to Say Goodbye' were coming through the thin walls from the well-used gramophone. As detached as he thought he was, the irony was not lost on him.

He knew the law, of course he did. With any luck, they'd be on to her straight away, maybe give her and the brother a hard time afterwards. Way back, he knew for sure, she'd have wound up in court, even been thrown out onto the street. He'd read all about it in the newspapers when he was a much younger man, after the first war, when it seemed everyone was either wounded or failing to get back on their feet, only for the same crushing catastrophe to engulf them all two decades later.

Yes, he'd come through two world wars relatively unscathed. Before that, so long ago, the big decision: to leave home, in Vitebsk, near the Russian/Latvian border. For good. No more being spat on, reviled because they were dirty Jews. They'd had a difficult time on the boat coming over. His wife, heavily pregnant, had given birth to their first child on the journey, a tiny miracle of survival; it could have so easily gone wrong.

He'd brushed aside his young wife's sorrow at leaving all she knew behind, determinedly repeating the mantra: 'It's a better life for us.' No more living in fear as despised outcasts, the lowest in the pecking order. Their new country was respected by everyone for its tolerance. The English were civilised.

Fifty years of life in the civilised country. There'd been no welcome, of course, but you blended in, just the same, because the everyday Londoners seemed, mostly, too concerned with themselves, too busy surviving, working, living, to trouble themselves too much about who or what you were. Or why you were there.

The upper crust, of course, looked down on everyone, let alone immigrants like them, but he'd taken pride in the way he'd organised it all, mastered the language, started work as a tailor and cutter, found a place to rent in Kensington; he was soon striding the smarter streets, measuring up the fine ladies in Harrods, creating their elegant tailored outfits.

But they were still a growing family, still Wandering Jews, as the children came, year after year, before the First World War, then during the Depression, the tougher times of the Twenties.

At first they'd spent many years in west London, but as his work waxed and waned, they'd wound up over the river in Greenwich above a baker's shop, then it was back over the river again to the East End for a couple of years, drifting to the slightly more respectable roads of Upper Clapton, all the while working hard, determined to keep it all together. Raising their kids in the Russian way: the boys indulged, waited on, the girls expected to help run the home. At one point, they'd even employed a servant. Then later, when things got tougher, he was thankful the girls were older, could work, bring something in. In London, if you kept working night and day, somehow you would get through. Even with a wife and eight kids.

By the time the second war started in 1939, he was in his late sixties, technically an old man, still sprightly and energetic, as proud of his smart-suited appearance as ever. Still working if he could, still the ladies' man, too, grabbing opportunity where he could find it with streetwalkers – too many of them now, especially in the middle of London – and in Leeds too, where they'd fled to twice: once during the Blitz, then again towards war's end, this time running away from the V1 flying bombs and V2 rockets, his wife already fading fast.

She didn't survive to witness the peacetime celebrations.

What made him, widowed at seventy-six, marry a woman thirty years his junior? It wasn't love. He hadn't loved his first wife, though she was an attractive, slender young girl when he'd first been introduced to her; it was an arrangement, as was the custom with their families.

But through the fixed, immovable, painful hostilities of his first marriage – her frequent rejection of him physically, until the times were such that he could not stop himself from forcing himself on her – he felt himself permanently cursed by the knowledge that she'd never wanted him in the first place, had loved another man and silently kept on loving him still. Forty-five years married – yet he had never been able to come to terms with that other unseen presence in their lives.

After he'd buried her, a return to London was out of the question. Where would he live without work and the place bombed to bits? His children were either back in London or scattered across the globe. His eldest girl, unmarried and in her fifties, would, of course, remain with him here in the North, play unpaid housekeeper as she'd done for so long while the other children grew up.

Then came the shock. His eldest girl had ideas. At nearly fifty, she found an advertisement in a local newspaper, wrote off for a pen pal. Then announced she was marrying him, a widower, older than her, but respectable. He'd stood there, stiffly, unsmiling, alongside the couple at the registry office in Wakefield. What now for him?

He found his answer at the Mecca Locarno in Leeds a few weeks later. Two and six to get in on a Sunday evening. He looked much younger, he knew, dropped ten years off his real age when he strode up to her. Far too much rouge, big hips, big bosoms, not his taste at all. But no resistance at all when it came to what he wanted. The rougher, more urgent he was, the more she seemed to like it. He knew the tarts faked their pleasure – he wasn't a fool, like most men – but he convinced himself this was no act to massage his ego. Yes, she wanted to know exactly how much he'd put by, which irritated him. But... there'd been a war, hadn't there? Everyone had been dragged through it. He'd worked a bit when war broke out, not much coming in afterwards. But he'd carefully saved, just the same, and with the new State pension they'd introduced in 1948, although not generous – just over £5 a month – meant he was a bit better off than many others.

He should have seen a warning sign when he met her stepbrother, a weaselly faced, sly, ignorant sort of lad in his twenties who claimed he'd seen out the war in the Fleet Air Arm, though he was suspicious as to the truth of this.

The stepbrother – she'd been raised by a big family who'd taken her in when her father died young – barely spoke to him. He shrugged it off, so caught up was he with the idea of a willing bed partner at home, someone who'd see him through to the end.

She'd had a much tougher life in the North than he or his family had ever known in London. But whatever their feelings, his oldest daughter and her new husband stood there, nonetheless, at the same Wakefield registry office a few months later. He'd move into the house she shared with the brother. Yet another consequence of post-war loss and chaos: people had to find comfort, anything, even if it just meant a home and respectability.

His chance to tell someone about the dreadful beatings by the brother, the constant demands for his money, rifling through his pockets when he'd return from the Post Office, the cruel complicity of the pair of them, came about a year after the wedding. A younger daughter, Sarah, wrote to him.

She wanted to come up briefly from London to say goodbye. She had a friend in Leeds to visit who'd put her up for the night, then she could meet with him. Best to meet at the station. She'd been widowed late in 1944, married just a matter of weeks. Now she'd found a distant cousin in Brisbane to sponsor her emigration overseas. She'd be leaving for good the following week, sailing off on an assisted passage from Tilbury where she'd board the SS *Ormonde* for the long six-week sea journey.

In the busy café in Leeds, they'd gulped down their strong tea and he found himself blurting out the truth about the violence, the beatings, unable to stop himself, deeply ashamed to find himself weeping at one point.

Typical of most Edwardian fathers, he had never been close to any of his children. As they grew into adulthood, their mother had made no secret of her loathing for him, the misery his physical demands made on her and the girls, not surprisingly, had taken her side to the last.

His daughter listened, wordlessly, but made no attempt to hug or comfort him. She was going. He'd half-hoped she'd have a suggestion, an idea, because she was a bright girl, a civil servant in Downing Street and then Berlin before deciding, like so many, to leave her past in a shattered Europe and take a chance, find something better in a faraway place. But there were no suggestions. In the end, it was a polite, restrained farewell inside the noisy station as she boarded the train. She'd write. He wished her well. Hadn't he done exactly the same thing, all those years ago? But his own drama, his shattered pride, weighed heavily upon him as he made his way back to the tiny terraced house that had now become his prison.

And so, in the chilly kitchen, the old man didn't pause for one final reflection on what he was about to do.

He didn't write a note. What was the point?

In a sense, he'd been on the run most of his life, a Jew, one of millions, running away from persecution and prejudice, then scuttling away from the wartime chaos with all the other Londoners, hoping for a safe haven. He and his children had survived: the lucky ones.

His pride in his minor everyday achievement, working night and day, raising a large, respectable family, had sustained him throughout. As a young man contemplating his fate, he'd long admired the British and their ways and, in fairness, the country hadn't let him down, turned against him. He'd been right to come here. Look what had happened to those millions who hadn't made a run for it when they could. He'd even become a naturalised British citizen two years before.

His last thought, as he stood up and made his way towards the stove and the gas tap, was a strangely comforting one: at the very least he would be ending his life as an Englishman...

My seventy-nine-year-old Russian grandfather's suicide in 1951, turning on the gas tap on the kitchen cooker and putting his head in the oven in the house he shared with his second wife, was a shocking family secret.

I knew nothing about it for most of my life.

It was only revealed to me by my cousin, Karen. Her father, Syd, one of my mother Molly's four brothers, had told her the story not long before he died in 2005.

Karen and I saw each other rarely. So it wasn't until 2010 when we visited the cemetery in Surrey where Syd and Molly are both buried that I heard the sad story.

I had never known my mother's parents. She had seven siblings but they had not turned out to be a close-knit family: indeed, I never even met three of her siblings.

Molly's mother, Bella, had died in Leeds in the spring of 1945, weeks before the end of the Second World War, following a painful death from breast cancer.

For as long as I could remember, that story, so traumatic for my mum who had helped nurse her mother, had been repeated to me, again and again by Molly, who adored her mother. As I grew up, I knew that Molly's father too had died in the north of England sometime after the war. But that was all I knew.

I was as shocked as anyone would be to learn of this other story, a secret concealed for decades. From early childhood, Molly had told me quite a bit about her past life. She was far from a secretive person.

She'd told me how she'd met my dad Ginger, five years her senior, at a dance in Clapton, East London, the area where both their families lived at the time. How they'd courted in those years of the late Thirties, only to find war breaking out and my dad's call-up more or less nudging them into a registry office wedding in 1940. How she'd remained in London through the Blitz, working in an Oxford Street shop, selling ladies' underwear. And how I'd been born in a castle turned maternity home, outside Leeds, just before war ended with Ginger far away in India, serving in the Pay Corps. Molly, two sisters and their parents had fled north suddenly when the V1s – the awful 'buzz bombs' – and the silent, far more deadly V2s started terrorising Londoners in the spring of 1944.

Wartime stories like ours, of course, echoed those of millions, recounted to successive generations down the years. Nevertheless, our families didn't get the very worst of it, not at all. Other families lived with grief, sudden widowhood, leaving mothers to raise small children alone. Or they faced the loss of loved ones killed by bombs and explosions in their own homes, often struggling afterwards to live with husbands and fathers returned from combat either physically or mentally shattered, unable to resume civilian life at all.

Nonetheless, my dad Ginger had 'a good war' by his own admission, a clerical job (thanks to a childhood eye injury) that only saw him posted overseas to India early in 1944, the final full year of war. His brother Nev was dispatched to Burma, which was a tough campaign, but he too came through relatively unscathed. Aside from my mother's sister, Sarah, widowed at the end of the war after just a few weeks of marriage, no one in either of my parents' families had lost a loved one or was badly injured or killed by bombings, even though both families had remained in London's East End for most of the conflict.

I grew up hearing about this. So when I finally heard about my grandfather, I immediately understood why Molly had deliberately chosen not to tell me what had happened to him. By then, I knew that in those days, topics like a suicide in the family were a secret shame, unlikely to be discussed openly.

So much that we discuss freely nowadays was unspoken of back then: divorce, illegitimacy, illnesses like cancer, tuberculosis, same sex relationships, suicide, the list was long. A stiff respectability, even if you lived frugally or modestly, back in the early Fifties was what counted. After the chaos of wartime, a somewhat stifling post-war world of conventionality had somehow taken over everyday life. So many family secrets lay, like ours, deeply buried in the rubble of the wreckage still acutely visible on Britain's landscape at that time.

Many children born out of wedlock in the war, for instance, grew up believing that the older 'sister' that took so much trouble to raise them was, in fact, their birth mother. Once the war had ended, it was often easier to live alongside a lie in morality-stricken early-Fifties Britain.

In 1951, when my maternal grandfather killed himself, me and my mum and dad, Molly and Ginger, were living amidst the mean streets of Hackney, London, bordering the notorious East End with all its crime, grit and poverty. We certainly didn't inhabit some polite, neatly manicured suburban enclave surrounded by relentless curtain-twitchers.

Yet our squalid surroundings made no difference at all when it came to keeping family secrets. Whispered gossip between neighbours, oh yes. Gossip about others' misfortunes or misdeeds was always neighbourhood currency – it hasn't changed much even today. But frank and open exchange within the family about an old man's desperate suicide? Unlikely.

In 1951, suicide was a crime.

An attempt at suicide that ended in failure could spell prosecution, even imprisonment for the survivor. And, bizarrely, a failed attempt could even be punished judicially with the death penalty. In some cases, even the families of those who had succeeded could also be prosecuted. My grandfather, Harris Richter, surely knew this.

Such was the silence I grew up with around his ending, it was only after I'd researched his life more and checked online records that I discovered his name was not even 'Oliver', as I'd believed in the past. My mum had talked of him, but never mentioned his first name: it was one of her sisters, Rita, who had written an account of their childhood just before her death in Canada and who had, for unknown reasons, decided to name him 'Oliver'.

Domestic gas poisoning via turning on the gas kitchen tap was, back then, one of the most common ways of committing suicide. A relatively peaceful end from carbon-monoxide poisoning. Fortunately, in the mid-Sixties, when the source of Britain's gas changed from being derived from coal to natural gas (the lower levels of carbon monoxide in natural gas are unlikely to kill anyone), domestic gas was no longer the lethal household weapon it had once been. (Suicide itself was eventually decriminalised in 1961.)

Be that as it may, when I looked back to my early years and thought about it all, I summoned up, quite strongly, a vivid memory, a time when I believe Molly learned what had happened to her father.

By then, she had not seen him since the spring of 1945, when she returned with me to London following her mother's death. I'm not even sure if she corresponded with her father. It was easier then to let her older sister Jane, who remained up in Yorkshire after the war, write to her with any news. The more I focused on that morning in the summer of 1951 and the letter lying on our mat, the more I became convinced that as a child, I had witnessed the precise moment in time when Molly learned the truth.

Letters lying on the mat in the hallway were, of course, a very important part of people's lives then. As a toddler, I played with our big black Bakelite phone, CLIssold 2393 (the first three letters of a telephone exchange, rather than digits, were used in major cities until all-digit numbers were introduced in 1966) which sat on our living room windowsill. Home telephones post-Second World War were not commonplace at the time – only about 10 per cent of the population had a telephone then – so postcards and letters in the post remained a major lifeline of communication.

The other method of communication was the telegram, delivered by a boy on a motorcycle. In wartime, the sight of the telegram boy and his bike was frequently a harbinger of bad news. Through the Fifties, however, greetings telegrams remained extremely popular – mostly anniversary greetings and birthdays and it was popular for telegrams to be read aloud by the best man at weddings – until the telegram's demise in the Seventies. I always received a birthday-greetings telegram from my father's parents, Jack and Miriam. Never a card in the post.

My mother wrote regularly to her sister Sarah, who had remarried and was based in faraway Queensland, Australia. Her other sister Rita, living in Kenya, initially wrote – and sent parcels – to me as a tot: she'd made beautifully knitted, colourful cardigans and hand-sewn, pretty embroidered dresses for me, though these mysteriously stopped after the late Forties.

Throughout the 1950s, Sarah would also use sea mail (taking three months or more) to send us lots of magazines and journals, publications with big colour pictures and many food ads – still something of a novelty to us in early 1950s Britain.

Everything in those Aussie magazines seemed so bright and colourful, though they too had known wartime rationing of tea, sugar, butter and meat until 1950. Yet their pages revealed a world of sunshine, perfect, cloudless blue skies and juicy canned peaches, still a luxury for us at the time – unless, of course, you managed to score a supply of tins on the black or 'off ration book' market. Which we did.

Molly maintained somewhat intermittent correspondence with her oldest sister Jane up in the north of England. While she remained close to her sister Sarah throughout her life, there was a huge gulf between Molly and Jane, partly because of the big sixteen-year age gap, partly because Jane had long resented the fact that Molly, the 'baby' of the eight Richter children, had never been tied down by the rigours of housework and domestic duties around their family home, as Jane had been. Molly was pretty, engaging and had plenty of suitors even before my dad came on the scene. Jane didn't and remained single.

This infrequent correspondence from the North did contain

one post-war surprise, however, when Molly read that Jane, approaching the age of fifty, had forged a pen-pal relationship, via a newspaper advertisement, with a Yorkshire widower. The friendship had quickly developed and they'd married in 1947.

However, when my mother heard about this – after all, it must have been a magic moment for Jane to have acquired the married lady status so much later in life – it didn't seem to impress or please her overmuch. She had always felt sensitive to her oldest sister's jealousy of Molly's 'the baby doesn't do housework' status.

'I can just imagine what he's like,' she sniffed one day, discussing it afterwards with Ginger. 'A Northerner who smokes a smelly pipe and wears a shabby suit. Who'd want her? Only someone no one else wanted.'

I would never meet Jane so I have no idea how accurate my mother's description was. All I'd gleaned was that her childhood had given her the rough end of the stick in their family, tied to housework, having to run around, clean, wait on her four somewhat indolent brothers. She played the piano, I knew that.

My mum's was quite a musical and artistic family (music itself formed part of a very strong Russian family tradition) and Molly had learned the violin as a child. But she didn't draw, paint or write, though two of her siblings were artists: her sister Rita became a sculptor in later life.

So it was Sarah and Sarah alone with whom my mother corresponded regularly throughout her life. Sarah valiantly corresponded with relatives and friends back in Europe too. From faraway rugged Cairns in Australia's north, with its deadly tropical heat and even deadlier insects and crocodiles, Sarah wrote to Molly saying she was as enthusiastic about this unexpected development in their oldest sister's life as my mum was unimpressed.

'Molly, he's a very nice man, retired,' she wrote. 'He was a factory foreman for most of his life, he and his wife never had any children and he seems to suit Jean well.'

But to Molly, an East End bookie's wife who'd once sat behind Princess Elizabeth at the theatre, went on seaside holidays in a chauffeur-driven Daimler and loved nothing more than to dress up and twirl around the dance floor in a shiny new dress, this kind of stuff was irrelevant. Respectability counted, of course it did. But only up to a point: Molly and Jane were chalk and cheese, not just years apart. It was as simple as that. The rivalry between the pretty baby whom everyone petted and the sour-faced drudge was immovable.

Yet on that Saturday morning, the letter from Jane that arrived on our hallway mat contained news none of the sisters expected.

'It's from Yorkshire!' I announced, running into the bedroom to deliver it to Molly, who was sitting facing her ancient wooden dressing table – complete with dark green-backed dressing table set of brush, mirror and comb – attending to her morning ritual: applying Max Factor Pan Stik, bright red Cyclax lipstick, smartening herself up for the leery stallholders of Ridley Road who couldn't give a stuff that Cyclax cosmetics bore the Royal Warrant – yet to millions like my mother, the endorsement alone gave a cheap sixpenny lipstick huge cachet.

Even then, make-up brands deployed celebrity as prime pulling power. Royal celebrity, at that time, was the ultimate marketing ploy: the wedding of the then Princess Elizabeth to Prince Philip in November 1947 had provided a much-needed rare ray of dazzling light to the millions still stuck in Britain's murky and depressing post-war gloom.

I had immediately recognised Jane's sloping handwriting on the envelope as well as reading the Wakefield postmark. Molly took it from me and tore it open to digest the contents while I hovered by the dressing table, curious as ever.

Silence. Not a word. Very unusual. None of the 'oh she makes me sick', the dismissive, sharp comments about her sister. Nothing. Then I realised: my mum looked funny, a bit strange. Despite the make-up, the colour seemed to have gone from her face. For a moment she just sat there, silently, staring out of the bedroom window. Not like my mum at all.

Even before I could open my mouth to say, 'What's it say, Mum?' or ask one of my interminable questions, Molly folded the letter, shoved it back in the envelope and headed, still clutching it, for our little kitchen, and closed the door firmly behind her.

This was something she never did.

But I didn't follow her or start nagging as to why she'd barricaded herself in the kitchen. My own childish concerns that morning were far more important: I planned to go to the library, find a new Enid Blyton book about the Famous Five. A voracious reader, my life virtually revolved around school and finding new books to read.

My mum's mostly negative comments about her sister had more or less convinced me that there was nothing really interesting to know about this woman, living in the far off, seemingly frozen north of England.

I'd absorbed my mum's many stories about the harsh, freezing winters up there the year I was born just outside Leeds. Cold places could only spell misery to me. We'd already lived through the terrible freezing winter of 1947 in London, and although I was a toddler at the time, I'd heard enough snippets of talk about it to understand that cold weather was Our Enemy. Even now, it was bad enough in winter stamping my feet to warm them up, jumping up and down as I waited impatiently for my mum to buy the vegetables in Ridley Road and finish her daily chores, so we could get back home to the flat and the coal fire in the living room.

Jane died in the Sixties, taking the story of the secret contents of that letter with her to the grave. Sarah, in faraway Australia, must have received a similar letter from Jane telling her the bad news about their father when it happened. Be that as it may, she too didn't, couldn't, share the contents with those around her.

Had my mother and two of her siblings not lived until their nineties, I might never have known the story. Right to the end, Sarah remained sharp with an excellent memory. She still managed to write to me sometimes not long before she died in 2008, even though her writing was pretty shaky. As sisters, Molly and Sarah were close: so my relationship with my aunt retained the imprint of that closeness.

After hearing the story, I emailed Sarah's daughter, Julia, in

Sydney. I didn't doubt what Syd had told his daughter, but he was gone and I still hoped to find Sarah's take on it all. Had she confided in her daughter?

She had, not long before she died. Like me, Julia's knowledge of the Richter family had many gaps. She hadn't even known that her mother had arrived in Brisbane, Australia as a war widow. Another family secret.

It was only when Julia, by then in her late teens, had discovered her mother's Second World War wedding photo, taken with her late husband Anton, killed late in 1944 in a bombing raid on a cinema in Antwerp, that she had confronted Sarah, who had recounted the story of her widowhood. (Sarah's second husband had forbidden her to tell anyone she'd previously been married, such was the rigid conservatism of the environment they lived in then.)

'Mum knew she didn't have long to go and we had a really long talk one day and I asked her everything I'd always wanted to know about her family, but never dared mention,' Julia told me.

In the end, Sarah didn't flinch. She told her daughter the story of our grandfather's remarriage and suicide. Yes, he'd been lonely and isolated after Jane married. So he'd remarried a woman of forty-seven in Wakefield, a woman of dubious reputation. The marriage had proved to be a terrible mistake, his new wife and her half-brother violent bullies. They took whatever they could from my grandfather's meagre pension and savings, treating him with callous brutality.

Today we call it elder abuse. Families set up hidden cameras in their parents' homes to record similar acts of cruelty or theft. By all accounts, my grandfather was far from a helpless, bed-bound invalid. He'd remained fit and active. Yet his last years had turned into a living hell.

'You couldn't talk about suicide, people didn't dare speak about such things then,' Sarah told Julia. I thought if I did tell anyone, they'd think there was mental illness in our family.'

But if the shame around our grandfather's suicide had compelled her to stay silent for so long, Sarah had also been haunted by the memory of their last meeting too: 'It was awful watching him cry, knowing I couldn't do anything. I was booked to sail away just a few days later,' she told her daughter.

Resourceful to the last, with nowhere to run and his family scattered all over the place, Harris Richter, proud, independent, but ultimately weakened by age and circumstance, had taken the only recourse possible. He'd chosen his own ending.

However, the two sisters who shared the family secret hadn't said a word to anyone. I don't even think Molly confided in my dad, though even if she had, he would also have seen it as something to stay shtum about. He too had barely known Molly's father, though her mother, Bella, had very much approved of Ginger in the couple's courting days. His cheeky Cockney humour had appealed to her.

As for me, I was close to seven years old on the day that letter arrived, an inquisitive bookworm, a spoilt, overprotected only child dedicated to reading, writing, regularly haunting our local libraries in Dalston Lane and Farleigh Road for Enid Blyton and, later on, books by a writer called Jean Plaidy who wrote many fictional historical novels in the Fifties and Sixties. (Plaidy's real name was Eleanor Burford, an East Londoner who had been inspired to write historical romantic fiction through growing up in London, surrounded by so much of the city's history.)

I'd been getting top marks in school, Princess May Primary, which was housed in a big Victorian building perched amidst the drab and sooty bombed-out surrounds of what is now known as the A10 or Kingsland High Street. The school was a short walk from our flat on the third floor of a small red brick Thirties block of flats with a strange turret shape.

Princess May was a girls' school with big classes of forty-five kids, most of whom were from solidly working-class homes, but not exactly ' snotty urchins' as Molly dubbed the attendees at my first primary, Colvestone Crescent.

Molly had insisted that I was removed from Colvestone, close by the Ridley Road street market, after a year or so because it was 'too rough' a mixed primary, which Molly believed was doing me no favours. Ridley Road was a ten-minute walk from our street, so there was an obvious advantage of me being even closer to home. (As for the urchins of Ridley Road and Colvestone, I bear no scars. Or even painful memories.)

Our little street ran in between Shacklewell Lane and Arcola Street. It was, even in 1951, a testament to the power of Hitler's ambitions. At the Arcola Street end of the street stood the boarded-up remains of a bombsite which had gradually morphed into some sort of car yard over the six years we had lived there. On the Shacklewell Lane end was a badly damaged house, still inhabited. Next door to our block were the remains of two bomb-damaged cottages, also still inhabited. And directly opposite our block of flats was a noisy timber yard, newly emerged from the wartime rubble and growing busier each year as restrictions lifted and the demand for building materials gradually started to materialise.

Technically, we were living in Hackney, E8. Or, if you wished, you could call it Dalston, E8, since Dalston Junction was less than half a mile away. But across the Kingsland Road, it was Stoke Newington, N16. We were on the borders, as it were.

Not that the postcode mattered then. Today, Stokey, as its known fondly by its inhabitants, is a very fashionable, gentrified area. Neighbouring Hackney too, reinvented and reborn, has scaled the ladder of desirability: it was recently touted as one of London's most expensive boroughs. People live there with pride at having landed in this colourful, historic area. Plans are afoot to create a conservation area around some parts of Hackney.

Yet back then, conservation would have been an unknown concept for Hackney's residents. Kingsland High Street, admittedly once a bustling, prosperous Edwardian thoroughfare, was then a miserable, shabby enclave, lined with dingy shops where women in headscarves, drably clad in Pakamacs (the foldup plastic 'raincoat in your pocket') or wartime utility coats and hats still stood in the rain, patiently queuing with ration books and coupons. (All food rationing didn't finally end until 1954.)

Clothing shops on the street and in the windows of the big department store, Dudley's, sported dull, uninspiring outfits (clothing too was rationed until 1949, and large-scale clothing manufacturing didn't get into its stride until the mid-Fifties).

Red trolley buses and taxis ran along the Kingsland Road but by today's standards there were few cars, other than the odd Morris Minor (priced at £358 when it was first launched in 1948) or the slightly pricier Standard Vanguard crawling along. Petrol rationing had ended in 1950, yet like so much else, large-scale car manufacturing didn't really get going until the mid-1950s.

Everywhere you looked, then, it was grey, cheerless, with a depressing overhang of post-war deprivation.

Trees and abundant greenery didn't feature much in this landscape. The nearest green open space was Hackney Downs, a twenty-minute walk from our flat. There kids could play, run free in the open air. But I never did: the Downs had been the setting for a traumatic event for me: I always shrank back in fear whenever a dog came into view on the street because one had leapt up and knocked me down as a tiny tot on the Downs. Well, that was the story everyone heard from my mum.

In the surrounding streets, apart from one big council estate called Hindle House, built in the late Thirties as part of a slum-clearance programme, stood old Victorian houses, either dilapidated or bomb damaged, many of them quite large, without bathrooms, often housing two, three or even more families.

Some families took in lodgers, renting out shabby, uncarpeted, chilly rooms that had somehow escaped the worst, simply to bring in enough to scrape by. Married couples often had no choice but to live with their parents; in some cases you'd find all three generations under one roof in homes that often had outside toilet sheds in the mostly neglected gardens. A few families then were homeowners, but London's post-war landlords, always greedy since time immemorial, were charging far too much for housing that was sub-standard, just about fit for habitation. Far too many people then remained living in war-damaged homes, still waiting for the council to rehouse them.

'The war? Ah, you just got on with it, love,' was the refrain of those locals who'd had no choice but to stay put, tough it out. They'd survived. Still, here they remained in battle-scarred Hackney.

Millions across the country were still 'getting on with it' in those days of my early childhood as Britain – damaged, broke and uncertain what victory meant –slowly staggered to its feet again: theirs was a mostly drab existence, of continued rationing, harsh winters, bad housing and hand-to-mouth living.

Okay, so there were no more bombs, no more air-raid sirens and fewer sing-songs around the pub piano about 'Itler having just one ball. Yet, for that early part of the Fifties, at least, to many it didn't really seem like the war was even over…

CHAPTER 2

THE ELEVEN-PLUS

Trafalgar Square,
London, 4 July 1954

Flashbulbs pop at midnight and ration books are ceremoniously burnt as the country celebrates the longed-for moment: the end of all types of food rationing. It is nine years after the Second World War ended and fourteen years since rationing began.

For millions, this is a long-awaited day. Buff or green ration books (the green ones were for pregnant women and mums of under fives) had dominated family life for far too long.

Yet I don't recall seeing a ration book in our home. For us, everyday life was far away from the world of scrimping and saving, moaning about the rations or worrying whether the bills or rent would be paid. We weren't waiting for the local council to determine our fate, either. Yes, we were living in a noisy, poky rented flat with paper-thin walls, tiny coal fires and, for the first few years of my life, no running hot water, rent just £1 a week from a private landlord. But as far as my dad Ginger was concerned, we were beneficiaries of the good life.

We certainly had everything we needed – and then some. All the food three people could possibly eat, seaside holidays in smart hotels each year (driven down to the coast in a chauffeur-driven Daimler), delivery men from Petticoat Lane bringing big carrier bags crammed with food and goodies from the Lane's busy market right to our door, a babysitter, a cleaner, as many smart cocktail dresses, outfits, coats and strappy platform shoes as my mum could cram into her wardrobe. And me decked out like a little curly haired princess in snug, the softest of wool coats with contrasting velvet trim, pretty organdie or puff-sleeved seersucker dresses and beautifully knitted Fair Isle cardigans.

How come, when everything around us screamed slum? Well, strictly speaking, the Hyams family of E8 lived off money earned outside the law. Not quite criminal. But very nearly bent, teetering on the edge. Welcome to bookieworld.

My dad Ginger worked with his father Jack, running their betting business just off Petticoat Lane in the hub of London's East End.

My grandfather Jack (or 'The Old Man') was what was known then as a 'commission agent' or 'turf accountant', a bookmaker legally permitted to take bets on the gee-gees or the dogs – or anything else people wanted to bet on – because he was licensed to operate from an office, where punters could run their own credit account, phone in and place their bets.

In the Fifties, there were only two places where bookmakers

could legally take bets: either from an office like the one my grandfather and dad operated at 11 Harrow Place, off Middlesex Street E1 (phone number: BIShopsgate 5000), where their punters phoned in bets and ran an account or, if bookmakers chose, they were allowed to work outdoors at the races or the dog track. Any other kind of betting, i.e. on the street or in the pub, was strictly illegal.

Nonetheless, a great deal of illegal betting thrived over the country, not just in the thick of London's East End. Such bets were taken mostly in pubs and on the street with 'runners' employed by the bookies to take the betting slips or cash back and forth between punter and bookie.

It had all been going on for a long, long time. The shop itself in Harrow Place had been in the Hyams family for over a century, morphing over the years from a home-removal operation (hiring a man with a horse and cart to move your belongings) into a shop selling coal, until my granddad decided to turn it into a bookmaking enterprise.

If bookies were caught trading the illegal way, there were heavy fines and court appearances. But of course, in a place like the East End's 'Lane' with its long history of duckers and divers, those who saw the law as a flexible concept could often thrive.

What kept it all kosher for illegally inclined off-track bookies like Ginger and his dad was their use of the 'bung' (a cash handout or tip), making sure the local constabulary were given a regular cash stipend to keep quiet about the illegal street or pub bets, so that the business itself ran along quite smoothly. Loadsamoney for the bookies when they won, not so good for those regular punters whose compulsively persistent betting habit often left them and their families near destitute.

So through the late Forties and Fifties my grandfather and dad, known to his family as Ginger No. 1 (Ginger No. 2 was my dad's younger brother, Nev), were raking in the cash.

Betting was then, as it remains, enormously popular. Since the Twenties there had been the hugely successful football pools run by big companies like Littlewoods, Vernons and Zetters, where people could legally place relatively small amounts of money as bets on the outcome of that week's football fixtures, with the results announced on BBC radio's *Sports Report* (and later the telly) at 5 p.m. every Saturday. Across the country, millions would stop everything to see if they had chosen the magic winning eight score draws.

Thousands were employed by these companies to check the entries. By 1955, a whopping £74 million was being reaped by the football pools companies and, in 1957, pools collectors were employed to pick up entries and deliver winnings door to door.

'When we win the pools' became the slogan of the people, only to be replaced by 'when we win the Lottery' when the National Lottery was introduced in 1994.

In his tiny Harrow Place office, Ginger helped run the clerical side of the business for his father, taking the phone calls, noting down the legal bets in his neat handwriting, working out the winnings, taking and paying out cash when necessary – as well as overseeing the illegal side of the business for his dad. This side of the operation was run mostly from the bar of the George

& Dragon pub, situated just a short stroll around the corner in Houndsditch.

Ginger had briefly worked alongside his dad in the betting game before war broke out. So when he finally returned to civvy street in 1946 after his stint in Meerut, India, he opted to get stuck in again with his dad. It was easier. His dad was a well-established, respected fixture in the area, Ginger knew the terrain, and he had me and Molly to consider now. It was a cash-only venture, so he could earn great deal more than the average wage of £7 5s 6d a week back in 1950.

It's difficult to say precisely how much my dad earned as a bookie. Ever since I could remember he always had a chunky stash of red-brown 10-shilling notes, green one pound notes and black and white fivers (£5 notes) crammed into his wallet as he made the morning journey to the office, six days a week, along the Kingsland Road to Liverpool Street and Petticoat Lane returning home by black cab (fare: just under 5/- or five shillings) each night from the George or somewhere similar.

London's black cabs always loomed large in my childhood. Many East Enders still remember the clip-clop sound of the man with the horse and cart – the rag and bone man – from that Fifties era. For me, the sound of a black cab's diesel engine running from the narrow street below my bedroom window, while my dad paid the cabbie, remains one of my most vivid memories of childhood.

Smells too provoke a powerful sense of childhood – my memory of the annual Queen of the May festival at primary school is easily invoked by the scent of May flowers: the tiny wild flowers of the hawthorn tree, little white (or occasionally pink) highly scented flowers that appeared in May. Even in the midst of a bombed-out city.

Grandfather Jack was, by then, in his sixties, getting on. He'd still stand there at the bar in the George in his dark-rimmed glasses, big heavy overcoat and wide-brimmed hat, shouting drinks for the assorted cops, crims, journos, bank workers and stallholders that crowded the George's cosy bar.

The George in Houndsditch was part of the City of London, the Square Mile precinct. So the pub was effectively positioned at a junction of the two different worlds and classes, a place where the Cockneys of Petticoat Lane drank with the 'City gents', as the posh bank workers, complete with bowler hats and brolly, were known then. Most importantly for Jack and Ginger, this pub was where the City of London coppers went each night to down a quick pint or a double scotch. With his dad running out of steam (but not Johnny Walker's Black Label), much of the running of the post-war business had now been handed down to Ginger.

He didn't mind, in those days. Ginger positively relished the macho life of the East End bookie. He loved the raucous, witty one-liner-a-minute world of the knockabout Londoner, knew everyone in the thick of the Lane where he'd grown up. He was buddy-buddy with the notorious Kray Twins' dad, Charlie: Ginger and Charlie had once worked 'on the knocker' together (buying second-hand goods and old gold from housewives) along the South Coast as younger men in the Thirties, though in later years their relationship mostly took the form of the odd heavy-drinking session in Dirty Dick's, the Liverpool Street pub, as Charlie regaled my dad with stories of the twins' violence and criminality.

Ginger was fanatical about sport, especially soccer – he'd played it as a kid – and he loved boxing too, frequently attending all the big fights of the times.

Boxing, of course, has long historical links with London's East End. Immigrant groups of fighter, including Jewish, Irish, Italian and Afro Caribbean, from the area frequently turned out world-famous champions. In many ways, boxing was seen as an opportunity for talented youngsters, a chance to get away from the area's meaner streets and long-forged links with crime and thieving.

Ginger was always the first one to flash the cash and buy drinks for everyone in the George. The publican, Siddy Cohen, and his wife, remained close friends for years. And Jack was a generous bar-hopper too, the rationale being they had to keep the punters happy, didn't they?

As a result of all this, a great deal of the hard cash that flew into my dad's wallet through his successful betting endeavours, promptly flew out again to go... down the toilet, to put it politely. A drinker's life, six days a week.

Only on Sundays, the day when nothing much at all happened in Fifties Britain, did Ginger lay off with a brief lunchtime trip to the pub, then a lurch back home to spend the rest of Sunday sobering up, usually in bed, priming himself for the next week's boozing and betting marathon. His dad did more or less the same.

Perhaps some would say, 'What's not to like?' at this sporting, boozing endeavour. But the truth was, it was a man's world back then and this was pretty typical East End behaviour, part of the historical tradition of the area where authority was either to be shunned – or, if it suited your way of life, casually bribed.

Molly, for her part, didn't try to change anything or question this life on the edge of respectability. She was a happy woman, loyal to a fault. Ginger's boozy East End habits weren't anything like the life she'd known as a girl – pubs, for instance, were unknown to her until she met him – but she had me to love, dress up and fuss over, she didn't need to go out to work and there were no money worries whatsoever, unlike so many families living around us.

She could also indulge herself as often as she wished in her favourite activity: glamming up and adding more new outfits to the over-crammed wardrobe, usually made to measure by a local dressmaker called Irene. Girlie heaven. As a tiny tot, I'd stand there watching as Irene, her little velvet pad of pins by her side, measured and pinned-up the hems and sleeves of my mum's latest slinky garment.

So many of the fabrics or materials used then for made-to-measure clothing have now vanished from view or are ruinously expensive, if you can track them down. Organdie, taffeta, tulle, velvet, silk, beautiful delicate fabrics that underline femininity, long gone in a world of mass-produced clothing.

Yet there was so much pleasure to be found in wearing bespoke clothing. Mass-produced clothes had been on sale since the beginning of the industrialised world, but ordinary working-class women with limited resources usually made their own. So when the Second World War came and virtually all manufacturing ground to a halt for the war effort, they continued to do this, resourcefully using scraps of precious fabric, like parachute silk, to make undergarments, for instance. Or they'd knit or use pattern catalogues or sewing books. Most families had a mother or siblings who could sew really well, work the sewing machine or knit beautifully.

Homemade clothes then became part of the post-war 'make do and mend' culture, so dressmakers like Irene, working from home, continued to thrive throughout the Fifties and right into the next decade until mass-produced clothing for everyone really took off.

My parents stepped out frequently, usually to the West End, in the Forties and Fifties. Trips to see the latest musicals or shows, outings with some of my dad's flash punter pals, big East End knees-ups or family weddings, plenty of reasons for Molly to don her finery and dance, which she loved.

Being a bookie's wife didn't have status or social cachet per se beyond the Lane, a place where being either a publican or a bookie did give such individuals a certain amount of gravitas. The bookie had cash, the publican ran the bar, which meant they were very important people in the community.

Molly's girlfriend from her childhood years, Evelyn, safely ensconced in the outer greener suburbs, would tut and sneer at Molly's post-war good fortune, seeing it as a flagrant breach of the respectability everyone aspired to. But like the other wives of the owners of businesses around Petticoat Lane or the families of the busy, boisterous costermongers selling fruit and veg in the market, Molly understood perfectly that these East Enders' lively cash businesses were unlikely to ever see them 'go short', as they said in those days.

Many stallholders, of course, had done exceptionally well during the war, trading illegally on what was known as the black market, where off-the-rations goods, sourced from who knows where, could be flogged quietly to locals at a very good profit: one good reason why succulent canned peaches and many other goodies turned up in our flat frequently long before rationing ended. So successful was the black market that stolen ration books – in 1944 it was estimated that 14,000 were stolen from individuals and offices – would be sold off illegally for a fiver.

My mum and dad inhabited a world where tomorrow or the future didn't feature. They didn't hold the view that you should try to save or hoard money; it just wasn't in their repertoire. In my parents' world, there was no respect or reverence for what money, once hoarded or set aside, could do for you, how it could cushion your existence against the unexpected bad times, offer you security for the times ahead. Mortgages, savings accounts, insurance policies didn't impinge on my dad's world view – or indeed that of his father.

'The Old Man doesn't believe in those things,' my dad told my mum. So he, in turn, followed suit.

The general attitude was: 'Have it, enjoy it, you can always get more.' The world of the street chancer, I guess. Or the gambler.

Perhaps some of my parents' attitude was a consequence of surviving the confusion and chaos of wartime. So many lives had been turned topsy-turvy by war and deprivation, it was often difficult to readjust in those early post-war years. But I do believe my parents were quite well matched, despite coming from different backgrounds. Their shared instinct was to live for the moment. Enjoy what you enjoy.

My mum remained like that right to the last; it was part of her lively personality, drew people to her, and it sustained her throughout. Ginger would pay the heavier penalty, being a bloke, or a 'man's man', who just wanted to carry on doing what he wanted, oblivious to all health concerns or warnings.

Was it reckless, stupid to live that way? Or did they have the right idea? It's open to question. I often think we expect far too much back from the frenzied, access-to-everything, swift-swipe consumer world of today. Their generation, born around the Edwardian or *Downton Abbey* era, had lived their youth with the clichéd maxim of 'know your place' in Britain's class-ridden pecking order. They hadn't been raised to believe the world owed them: they accepted that you took life as it came. Whatever it threw at you.

However, they'd grown up quite differently. My mother's family, including her siblings, were mostly invisible when I was young. As we've seen, Molly's parents, Harris and Bella Richter, having fled the persecution of the pogroms in Russia, arrived in England around 1903. They stayed briefly in the East End, then they moved to West London and Notting Hill, moving around the city as the family expanded and Harris's working life as a tailor and cutter ebbed and flowed with the fortunes of the times.

Recently, I learned that Bella never managed to learn to speak

English properly and relied on her children to translate for her when necessary. This made her somewhat shy and reclusive too.

Although the couple were religious Jews, attending synagogue and observing all the traditional Jewish festivals, somehow their Jewish traditions did not survive as far as their children were concerned: by the time the Second World War ended, three of their eight adult offspring had abandoned all their religious roots and married 'out', that is to say, married non-Jews, which was frowned upon, even scandalous amongst the closely knit Jewish community at the time (another taboo topic, one which Jewish people preferred not to discuss openly). Although, as with all immigrant groups, those born into the new environment are bound to question or brush up against the deep-rooted traditions of the older culture.

Molly and her sister Sarah, the youngest two, hung on to their religious heritage. Until Molly married Ginger, who although from a Jewish family, too, didn't believe in things like lighting the Sabbath candles every Friday night or observing all the Jewish traditions, eating kosher food, going to synagogue. (Sarah remained a quietly observant Jew for the rest of her life.)

The Old Man's family had lived in London's East End since the early 1800s and along the way they had abandoned their roots and become anglicised. They'd eat Jewish food. They retained membership of a local synagogue in Sandys Row, Spitalfields (primarily because membership fees meant they would be entitled to a Jewish burial). But they never went there – and they'd happily tuck into the foods Jewish people are supposed to avoid like pork and shellfish.

As a result of all this, while I grew up in an area where many Jewish people lived, we didn't follow the religion itself. There was even a big synagogue around the corner from our flat. (Today it's a mosque, which tells the history of the area to an extent.) But we didn't attend any synagogue or observe the Jewish customs. Only our dining table indicated our heritage. Molly didn't seem to mind any of this, despite her Russian Jewish childhood. Bacon and eggs alongside lokshen (chicken) soup and chopped liver. She was adaptable, my mum.

We saw much of Ginger's family, mostly his parents Jack and Miriam, who by then were living out the twilight of their lives in the North Flats, Stoney Lane. These big blocks of Victorian flats were known as 'Artisans' Dwellings', big estates dotted all over London that were constructed in the late 1800s, to be rented to local workers in need of housing.

'The buildings,' as they were called, were right in the midst of Petticoat Lane, almost cheek by jowl with the father-and-son commission agent's office at No. 11 Harrow Place. (The dwellings were eventually demolished, though the complex that stands in their place today is named Petticoat Square.) My grandparents, like many other Jewish couples who ran a business in Petticoat Lane, had decamped to the leafier streets and big family houses of Clapton, near Springfield Park, in the Twenties. But when the Second World War broke out, Miriam had insisted they move back to the grimy East End and 'the buildings' while Jack continued to run his 'turf accountant' business in Harrow Place.

Right up until the late 1950s, Molly and I dutifully visited 'the buildings' to pay our respects to Ginger's parents every Sunday afternoon, rain or shine. We went on family holidays each year with Jack and Miriam, too. This relationship, as I went from toddler to teen, became a source of growing resentment for me. Especially the enforced visits to their flat.

There were several reasons for this. From a very early age, I'd developed an intense fear and loathing of the area where they lived, initially fuelled by my own vivid imagination when being marched by my mum through those dark, desperate, narrow East End streets to Jack and Miriam's first-floor flat.

Jack the Ripper had done dreadful things to women, I'd heard as a toddler. My dad even drank in one of the pubs, The Bell on Middlesex Street, where a Ripper 'unfortunate' victim, Frances Coles, was reputed to have drunk her last glass of beer. So our trolley bus route to their home, running all the way along the A10 to Liverpool Street taking us past The Waste (a scruffy street market), the big St Leonard's hospital (now a block of posh apartments), the Geffrye Museum (originally built in 1714 as an almshouse for the poor, and still there, thankfully), and on to bombed-out Shoreditch (now Trend Central), then past Itchy Park, the fabled tramps' or dossers' habitat, finally to alight at Middlesex Street (Petticoat Lane), all made for a sooty, dank and depressing journey in those early post-war years.

The nineteenth-century history of the area around Middlesex Street is an oft-told one of poverty, alcohol, prostitution and desperate living in filthy, vermin-infested surrounds. So when we alighted from the bus at Dirty Dick's pub and embarked on the walk along Middlesex Street, then down to Stoney Lane, while it couldn't have been more than a six- or seven-minute walk through the deserted streets, the grim atmosphere of its history seemed to cling, determinedly, to every Dickensian damaged building, mingling with the wreckage of the post-war gloom. Those dark, sinister narrow streets were, to me, quite terrifying. It wasn't a stretch to imagine a gloved hand reaching out amidst the gloom, knife aloft, poised to rip your guts out...

But making this unlovely journey all the time was not the only source of my unease. There was more to it than that. We saw my dad's parents week in, week out, yet my mum's family, dotted all over the place, were never made welcome in our home because Ginger was an incredibly possessive person: he just didn't like anyone coming to visit us.

I was never encouraged to invite friends round, for instance. Though, to be fair, by the time I had started to work out what my dad's world involved and developed a loathing for our depressing surrounds, I didn't particularly want to bring anyone into our little flat.

My mum was outgoing and had chummed up with quite a few other women during her single years as a saleslady in the West End. But Ginger viewed all mention of her female friendships with great suspicion. Her best friend, Evelyn, for instance, never once came round to visit.

'She's a bad 'un, that one' was Ginger's description of Evelyn who was attractive, hardworking and struggling to raise a son of my age, Donald, all on her own in the 'burbs.

She'd had a tough life: a girl with five brothers, their mother had died in childbirth. She was very much a typical post-war single mum. Officially, Donald's dad had 'gone to live in Canada'. Well... maybe. No one then would openly admit to having a child out of wedlock because of the shame such status carried. A divorced woman bringing up kids alone faced the same kind of opprobrium. Women really were living in the Dark Ages back then. My mum did keep up one or two friendships with local women, now married, in the area. But she'd learned not to chat about them in passing to her husband. It was easier.

Ginger knew about Evelyn's story, of course, so that definitely made her little more than a woman of the streets, a tart, to use the expression of the times. Yet she'd have still have been unwelcome anyway, despite her history. Molly's siblings that did live outside London – her brothers, two of whom I never ever met – soon got the message: they simply weren't welcome chez Ginger.

Only Molly's brother Syd, easy-going and garrulous, would blithely ignore my dad's possessiveness. He'd just knock on our door, out of the blue. But that happened rarely, once every couple of years, if that.

We were, in many ways, quite isolated, my mum and I, in the cramped little flat.

Few visitors and an excess of Jack and Miriam in the Lane. Fortunately, I became an avid reader from early childhood, so I could escape into my damp little bedroom with library books and the magazines I later started to buy frequently. It was all very claustrophobic aside from the freedom of my imagination. And I was dedicated to schoolwork. Neither parent particularly encouraged me. It was just... there.

Until, of course, I started to reach my teens...

It's a Sunday afternoon in early 1955 and I am standing on the landing outside my grandparents' front room.

Their 'dwelling' is, essentially, made up of what had once been rented out to two families: the front room and a back bedroom leading off it, both facing the street below, make up the main half, the place where they do most of their living.

Out on the landing is a toilet cubicle, complete with wooden seat and scratchy Izal toilet paper. (Thankfully my grandmother has now abandoned the newspaper strips she used to deploy following wartime shortages.)

Off the landing, there is also a scullery or kitchen area of sorts, and, leading off that, two other rooms, one a bedroom – into which I never ventured – and the other, perhaps also a bedroom but now usually used as a dining room when my grandparents host family meals.

There is no bathroom, not even a small one like ours with a newly installed temperamental Ascot water heater that doesn't work properly.

Jack and Miriam take weekly trips to the nearby public baths in Goulston Street, a short walk away, price sixpence. They'd done that all their lives: 'MORE HOT WATER IN NUMBER SIX!' (number 6 refers to the cubicle number) was a familiar cry from those weekly bath-time trips.

In Clapton, families like theirs – and my mum's – regularly used the Hackney Public Baths near Clapton Square, where my mum wistfully recalled buying a slice of bread pudding (or 'pudden' as they called it) from the little kiosk inside, price just one penny.

Today, though, Molly and I have climbed the sour-smelling stone stairs to find, as usual, Miriam in her shapeless printed dress and dark blue pinny, her greying hair pinned high on her head, tiny gold earrings in her pierced ears, sitting at the table, complete with its mysterious newspaper covering (she could well afford a decent tablecloth, yet I never saw one covering the table) with a huge scowl on her pink and white face.

She nods at us but does not speak or even offer a cuppa or a slice of cake, from Grodzinski's bakery, a plain cake with a yummy, sugary white icing topping. Jack lies behind the bedroom door. We can hear him snoring his head off.

Uh-oh. The scowl. The silence. We know the signs. They've either had an enormous barney and Miriam is still sulking – or she and Jack are having one of their lengthy and frequent standoffs where they ignore each other for as long as they can. This makes it very difficult to be around them. The atmosphere isn't just frosty: it's downright lethal.

There are three of them in the marriage – Miriam, Jack and The Pub: Miriam, aged seventy-five, is enormously jealous of her toy-boy husband, aged seventy. Just five years between them but sufficient to set up an enormous and ongoing insecurity on Miriam's part, an irrational fear of losing him; it's been a running sore in their lives almost since the day they married, creating rows and screaming matches throughout. The move from Clapton back to the East End during the Blitz was wholly driven by this terrible insecurity. By returning to 'the buildings' Miriam could easily keep an eye on Jack in his adjacent office.

So even now, no longer young, Miriam remains convinced

that she risks losing Jack to another woman. Her problem is that bookie Jack has always inhabited a world she cannot control. The Pub. The Drinking. The Hours When Jack is Not At Home. East End pubs, like most pubs then, were resolutely blokey: smokey, unhealthy dens where respectable women did not venture unaccompanied – only loose women or prostitutes frequented these places.

When they were much younger Miriam would ignore the conventions and often turn up in the pub to drag Jack home – a familiar sight around the Lane and an ongoing source of titters and gossip – storming her way through the bar to demand that Jack 'Come Home Now'.

Sometimes Jack would put his glass down and follow his abusive wife down the street, only for the fighting to erupt back home. But mostly their kids grew up in a hellish world of screaming, shouting and threatening behaviour. Jack was quite a mild-mannered bloke when sober. But once Jack had a drink inside him he would give as good as he got.

The oldest boys, Gingers 1 and 2, copped the worst of it, witnessing the violent rows and sometimes on the receiving end of a heavy-duty slap. Mostly, it was Miriam that would thump them, usually in frustration and anger at Jack's drinking.

The two girls, Deirdre and Doris, came off better; they managed to switch off from it all. As did the youngest son, George, born in the mid-1920s when the family had moved to the more pleasant confines of Clapton.

I've just been to the loo but I'm lingering, not rushing to go back into the living room where the atmosphere's so palpably tense. So I stand there, the door half open, and I hear my mum trying her best to chat to Miriam. They're talking about me.

'Ginge says Jac's definitely going to pass that eleven-plus exam, Mum,' Molly is telling her excitedly, trying to diffuse The Horrible Atmosphere. 'She's such a clever girl and she's so good at reciting and acting, so Ginge thinks we should be sending her to a stage school.'

'Aida Foster, that's the one,' snaps Miriam, unexpectedly up to speed on the educational opportunities around London, perhaps because she is, somewhat surprisingly, an avid reader of *The Tatler*, the posh people's magazine.

'It's in Golders Green, on the Finchley Road,' adds Miriam. 'The girls still get normal education but they also have classes in dancing or acting. The Alfred girl went there and she's doing really well.'

My ears really prick up at all this, of course. A stage school? No one's said anything to me.

We'd heard all about the 'Alfred Girl' from Ginger who was thick as thieves with the Alfred family, local publicans. Ginger had even brought home a signed photo of her, Sandy, a cute dark-haired girl in her teens with pigtails and a bright smile. A budding performer and singer, she'd even been on TV in *The Dave King Show* a few months before. (*The Dave King Show*, starring singer-comedian Dave King, ran on the BBC from 1955–8, then it went to ITV. Dave also had big hit records in the Fifties, including 'Memories Are Made of This' in 1956. His career faltered when he went to America and he never again quite reached the heights he had scored in the Fifties. He died in 2002.)

Yes, I am obsessed with getting good marks, top of my class for the last three years, spending my after-school hours reading, practising reciting or learning my lines for school plays. But I don't think I really want to follow in the steps of the Alfred Girl. I'm not really keen on this idea of 'stage school'. Perhaps I'd have liked the idea of it more if I'd known that *Picturegoer*, the British movie magazine read by millions, headlined Aida Foster as 'The World's Most Glamorous School'. But fortunately (for everyone) I know nothing at all about it at the time.

I do know straight away I wouldn't be good enough, anyway, that they're having themselves on. I can carry a tune, remember my lines and tap dance. I'd gone to dancing class round the corner from us at Miss Betty's on the Kingsland Road since age three. The truth is, though, I'm a bit of a show-off when you put me on a stage. I have always been like that – it's my instinctive love of words, the English language that compels me. I'm not in the least bit athletic. I also have very little competition on the learning front at my primary, where the classes are so big. I'd started reading early and I carried on doing nothing other than read or write much of the time. A swot, plain and simple. Not a budding telly star.

Most of the other girls at my school are from bigger, rowdier families, where kids often play out on the street. They play games like hopscotch (on a grid, chalked onto the pavement). Or there'd be group skipping with a long rope, chanting the favourite skipping chant of the time. At nearly eleven, with over-protective parents, I play the usual skipping games in the school playground – our favourite chant was: 'My mother said

I never should/ Play with the gypsies in the wood' – but I'm no tomboy. I've never ridden a bike. Or climbed a tree. There's the rough and tumble of the streets all around me, sure, with kids clambering on bombsites to play.

But I'm outside it, wrapped up in cotton wool, a little princess, far too cosseted for my own good, though to be honest, our narrow little street had never been really suitable as a playground for any kid.

Suddenly, I hear a thudding sound. A door closes. It's Jack's heavy tread as he strides from the bedroom onto the thinly covered wooden flooring of the living room. I know from previous visits that he's in his shirtsleeves, with elasticated sleeve garters (to stop the cuffs from getting dirty), a dark waistcoat and trousers, no tie.

''Ullo Molly, Jacky, alright?' he says.

'Yes, Dad,' says my mum. 'Er... Just telling Mum how Ginge thinks Jac should go to stage school.'

'Wot's 'e know?' says my grandfather, always ready to push his eldest son and heir down a peg or two. 'If she's clever she could go to City of London, that's the best one around 'ere.'

Oh dear. What the hell is City of London? Is it a stage school? I'm not particularly worried about doing this eleven-plus exam, though my two friends at school, Kathy Shilling and Sandra Holland from Prince George Road, seem to be worrying quite a lot about it. Exams, I believe, are my chance to show how clever I am (overconfidence was, back then, a big part of my repertoire).

After hearing all this, I wander back in, join the adults. I've heard enough...

Jack, for all his drinking habits, knew his manor really well. Long after he'd gone, I discovered he'd been a Freemason. He had donated regularly to local charities, and in directing my mum towards the possibility of City of London School for Girls, he did have a point. It was, and remains, a prestigious school with an excellent track record. There were scholarships from such schools available back then for bright kids from working-class homes who had passed the eleven-plus exam.

But all this well-meaning speculation about my future will prove to be chitchat, no more. Make no mistake: some youngsters did have a golden opportunity in the world I grew up in. Thanks to the big changes in Britain's education system in 1944, the new Education Act aimed to provide a fair education for everyone, raising the school leaving age from fourteen to fifteen in 1947 (it went up to age sixteen in 1972) and introducing the eleven-plus exam. (There had been plans to raise the school leaving age to fifteen in 1936, but when war broke out three years later, these plans were temporarily shelved.)

The age of eleven was considered to be the best time to assess a child's general intelligence, so the eleven-plus examination was, essentially, a grading exam to determine the best school to suit each child's ability.

If you got top marks, you could go to a grammar school, learn languages, Latin and chemistry. At sixteen, grammar school pupils could take the General Certificate of Education in several subjects at Ordinary or 'O' level. After that, if they did well in O or A (Advanced) levels, education continued until, possibly, university.

Those who didn't score as well in the eleven-plus were sent to a secondary-modern school to learn domestic science or practical subjects. The other alternative, mooted at the time the scheme was launched for those who didn't pass the exam, was technical college. But the hoped-for numbers of tech colleges didn't really materialise. So the majority of kids went off to a secondary modern.

As it turned out, to me the eleven-plus exam seemed relatively straightforward because so much of the exam was about testing kids' command of the English language. After the starting bell, there was a fifty-minute paper, then an English test, then after a short break there was a test for English composition.

'Describe an enjoyable outing' the paper said. I'd gone to the Tower of London one day with Sandra and my mum. So off I went, scratching away with my fountain pen, describing Traitors' Gate, the ravens, everything I could remember. (Ballpoint pens, or biros as we call them, didn't really become hugely popular until much later in the Fifties.)

Then came a maths test followed by tests for verbal and non-verbal reasoning skills. The verbal reasoning test, of course, was to test your command of English; the non-verbal was a sort of IQ test. Afterwards, I told my mum, 'It was easy.'

When the little brown envelope arrived to say I'd passed, Molly and Ginger took Jack's advice and I did get an interview for the City of London school. But I didn't get beyond the initial interview to the exam for the scholarship stage. I wasn't as clever as I, or my parents, believed.

While it seemed like a good idea at the time, the eleven-plus was gradually phased out by the Seventies, though a version of the exam is still in place in certain parts of the country for those hoping for entry to a grammar school.

Yet despite all the hopes for the eleven-plus, both the onset of puberty as well as the times we were living in were conspiring against my further education.

Around the same time that I sat down in Princess May to take the exam, far away, across the Atlantic, something quite phenomenal was happening. It would create a huge eruption for the times, send a shockwave around the world that was unprecedented in the history of music and entertainment.

Back in 1953, a slender, dark-haired, dazzlingly handsome eighteen-year-old with a singing voice unlike any other had walked through the doors of a Memphis recording studio. This unknown poor boy from the badlands of southern America was destined, with his voice and body, to stir the senses and emotional yearnings of billions of youngsters. Within just a few years, this man's musical talent – and erotically charged performance – would change the landscape for ever, a commercial phenomenon unseen till then – particularly by eleven-year-old girls whose preoccupations until that point were quite childish.

I read books, collected stamps (most kids did then), played board games like snakes and ladders and ludo, and, again like most kids, cherished a buff-coloured autograph book that I'd give to my dad to in which to collect signatures if he and my mum went anywhere remotely glamorous. The best I got were boxers, alas, but still, seeing 'To Jacqueline, best wishes from

Nicky Gargano' gave me some satisfaction since he was quite cute and dark-haired. (Nicholas Gargano was an outstanding young London amateur boxer, a welterweight champion in the Fifties who won a gold medal in the 1954 Commonwealth Games. He retired, aged twenty-two, in 1957.)

Recently I'd started to vaguely admire another dark-haired man – the dimpled actor Richard Greene in the ITV series *The Adventures of Robin Hood* (the series ran from 1955–9 and spawned a hit song with the immortal opening line: 'Robin Hood, Robin Hood, riding through the glen' in 1956), but I wouldn't describe this as a passionate crush, more an early hint that I'd soon have a proclivity for dark-haired men.

But boys? They weren't yet on my radar. How did you even talk to them? I didn't have brothers. I went to an all-girls' school. I didn't even play in the street with boys. I didn't live in a world where they seemed to matter. Yet.

Elvis, the voice and the image, would start to change all that, thanks to the release of a succession of 78rpm vinyl records and the huge publicity machine that cranked up following his first successes.

At precisely the point when my own future was supposedly determined by me scratching some words onto paper in a chilly Victorian classroom in Barretts Grove, Elvis – sensual, super shiny with that crazy, sexy Southern accent – had embarked on his own incredible journey into the lives of teenagers everywhere. And such was my growing fascination with him in the next year or so, in my mind he could have been driving his big pink Caddy along the 649 trolley bus route, past the grim bombed-damaged façades of Liverpool Street station and up the long, war-stained Kingsland Road.

Picture it: Elvis with his slicked-back hair, velvet jacket and sideburns, buying fruit 'n' veg in Ridley Road? Or strolling into the bagel shop for smoked salmon and cream cheese bagels. It's a compelling thought, one of many similar fantasies I would have about Elvis stepping out of his world so far away and right into ours.

Yes, it was only Elvis who would later lure an innocent, somewhat single-minded little swot far, far away from education or learning towards all the complex, churning emotions of the child turning into adult.

Culturally, as far as movies and music were concerned, it had always been a case of America led, we followed. Yet the shift from the popularity of the adult music of crooners like Sinatra, Tony Bennett, Frankie Laine or Johnny Ray around the mid-1950s to the breakthrough sound, the pounding rock 'n' roll beat of Bill Haley and the Comets' 'Rock Around the Clock' (and the follow-up 'See You Later, Alligator'), was dramatic.

This new music, with its vibrant abandon, a hybrid of rock 'n' roll and hillbilly (or country) music, became a clarion call for the young. Post-war teenage kids who couldn't wait to shake off everything their parents believed in. Until then, teenagers hadn't really existed in anyone's imagination as a separate entity.

In the States, the advertising and marketing gurus of Madison Avenue reputedly coined the word 'teenager' in the 1940s, around the time of the bobby-soxers, the young girls who visibly swooned over the youthful Frank Sinatra. So teenage culture in America, whose economy boomed immediately after the war ended, had already started to be exploited to stunning effect long before it hit the shores of Blighty.

Here, however, we were still expected to be clones of our parents, dress like them, dutifully follow them along the same path. Adolescence was not a widely accepted or over-examined state of affairs.

Mostly, it was ignored. One minute you were a kid, then mysteriously you were deemed grown up. Until the day the new music came and the marketing gurus here realised they'd been missing a trick. A very big one.

CHAPTER 3

THE WOMAN FROM CHATS

But I'm getting ahead of myself here. It wasn't only Elvis and the rock 'n' roll explosion that heralded change. By the time I took the eleven-plus exam, the country had just started to throw off the past, get on its feet. It was a slow process. But we were beginning to move ahead.

Ginger's wallet, as ever, was still crammed with the readies. We continued to live like lords in a squalid setting, thanks to the unrelenting passion for betting around the Lane and my dad's cosy relationship with the Old Bill. But despite all this, when it actually came to going out and buying things for our home, there still wasn't very much in the shops to buy, brand new, through the cold and smoggy years of the early Fifties.

Mass production of furniture had ground to a halt. Only when the restrictions on buying new furniture ended in 1953 and all forms of rationing ended the year after, did the shops dotted along the Kingsland Road start to stock brand new furniture and household items.

So while I was at Princess May, poring over my marks, eager to stay top of the class, dipping into a bag of Love Hearts or sucking on Sherbet Dip Dabs in the playground, Molly's daily trips to Ridley Road market took her past shop windows that were noticeably changing.

Back then, London boasted three evening newspapers: 'Star, News and Standard!' was a familiar cry on street corners. By the mid-1950s the newspapers too were filling up with advertisements for all sorts of consumer goods. The local papers – ours was the *Hackney Gazette* (which came out three times a week) – also started running big ads for the new furnishing items now readily available.

Andrews Furniture at Highbury Corner offered locals a 'walnut finish three-piece bedroom suite' – all for the price of £56, a mini revolution in home making.

My parents got one of these for their bedroom. Most of the furniture we had until that point was what they used to call 'utility' – very simple, a bit angular, for day-to-day living – sideboard, chairs, tables, all very plain.

My damp little bedroom (measuring about 10 by 8 feet) bang opposite the timber yard, had just a single bed with a plastic headboard and a pale beigey coloured wardrobe made out of some sort of inexpensive plywood, with an inbuilt small mirror. Later on, a melamine dressing table with two drawers and a swing mirror was also purchased from Bardens, a big furniture store on Kingsland Road High Street. My walls, originally covered in flowered wallpaper that had seen better days, were now repapered with a beigey plain paper and very bare – though they wouldn't stay that way for much longer.

Ginger had zero input, of course, into choosing what we had in our flat, other than just forking out. Yet Molly, while reasonably diligent when it came to food shopping, cooking and looking after me, wasn't exactly an obsessive homemaker, jumping for joy at the idea of a new pair of curtains or a set of brand new saucepans.

Most women then would sit down and make their own curtains – 2 yards of curtain material cost around 5s in 1952 – but my mum had our curtains made up for her, ugly beige floral ones from fabric purchased from a Ridley Road stall, to hang either side of the greying nets that protected us from the outside world.

A veritable network of women living near us were only too happy to earn 'the extra', making and putting up curtains, taking in washing and ironing, 'doing' for those who had the readies. Women like my mum's favourite dressmaker Irene, round the corner in St Mark's Rise, who as I've already mentioned was the creator of Molly's shiny calf-length taffeta dresses for nights out with my dad to see big West End shows like *Kismet* or *The Pyjama Game*.

Our very first fridge, complete with teeny freezer compartment at the top, was a revolutionary development, since we no longer had to keep things like meat, fish or milk in the old kitchen larder, which had once housed the blue bottles of free orange juice for me and the gold tins of powdered egg immediately after the war. It also meant there was no longer a real need to shop for food every day.

We had been fairly quick off the mark with the fridge. We got it just before Birds Eye frozen fish fingers were launched in Britain in 1955 (even then, just one in ten homes in Blighty boasted a fridge by 1957). I loved the fingers because I could 'cook' them myself, shoving them under the little grill at the top of the gas cooker, often managing to burn the corners in the attempt.

Be that as it may, curiously, with the big labour-saving items now becoming widely available, things like washing machines, dishwashers or even a brand new Hoover vacuum cleaner weren't seen as essential items in our home – probably because my parents 'contracted out' so much of our domestic requirement.

No washing and ironing of shirts for Molly – my dad organised the dry cleaning of his suits at the local Achille Serre, a large dry cleaning chain of shops across the country then, though now no longer in existence. He also got his shirts washed and ironed by someone in the Lane for many years. We had a regular, if somewhat useless, weekly cleaner called Annie who managed to break or damage more than she cleaned, using our not-very-effective Ewbank carpet sweeper. I don't think my mum believed we needed things like new machines to make life easier for her. By her standards, life was pretty easy anyway.

She looked after our clothes, of course. But my dad, who was obsessively neat and spruce in his habits, had picked up an iron discipline around his appearance somewhere along the line, maybe in Army days. So he took care of all his wardrobe requirements himself. A different suit each day, complete with crisply fresh shirt, smart tie, waistcoat, cufflinks, even braces. But, strangely enough, no hat, though both sexes frequently wore hats during the Forties and Fifties.

However, what was so daft about it all was that virtually all our new things for the home were purchased on credit or 'tick'.

Ginger was a devotee of the 'never never', or hire purchase, where you put down a small deposit, then paid off everything each week over a couple of years. Hire purchase on household items really took off in 1954 when the government reduced credit controls, though it is interesting now to recall that women were not permitted to sign such HP agreements themselves – only their husbands could sign.

My father could easily have handed over the full price for things like our new GEC fridge (priced at £66), but the idea of 'have it now, pay later' really appealed to Ginger (a trait which he successfully passed on to his daughter).

He didn't regard these household items as a priority in the general scheme of day-to-day living, so why hand over full price on the spot? My dad's attitude to credit was: if it's there, take advantage of it, use it to the max. This was fine in those golden illegal betting years of the Fifties; it would eventually prove to be less than useful once the industry went legit in the Sixties.

We were fast on the draw with the telly, too. We'd acquired our first-ever set in the months before the coronation of Queen Elizabeth in 1953. Until the coronation, very few people in Britain had TVs. But the coronation of the new, beautiful queen was such a massive event in people's glamour-starved

lives that once it was announced that it would be shown on
BBC TV, those who could buy, use HP or rent an early set went
out and got themselves a new Pye, Bush, Ekco or Ferguson for
the home.

Our 17-inch Ferguson TV from Bardens was priced at about
£70 (a big sum of money for times when the average weekly
wages tipped £11 a week in 1955), but Molly would happily
trot down the high street to pay off the 16/6d (sixteen shillings
and sixpence) weekly payment over two years.

Ginger, crazy for sport, had wanted a telly early on because
you could watch big sporting events on it (Coronation year's FA
Cup Final was shown on TV, but the most famous event on the
racing calendar, the Grand National, would not be broadcast
live until 1960), so it was really about Ginger's priorities rather
than any burning desire to be an early owner of brand new,
exciting technology.

Yet the acquisition of a TV by the masses proved to be a bit
hit and miss. Okay, we were lucky, we lived in London, but
other parts of the country didn't get TV reception at all until
quite a bit later. (Jack and Miriam, however, were Luddites: HP
or not, they rejected the new-fangled nonsense.)

In the very early years of BBC TV (commercial telly and ITV
didn't arrive in Britain until 1955) sets purchased way before
1955 often had to be replaced, since many of the earliest sets
could not broadcast both networks. You didn't get much of a
picture in those early years: viewers would often wind up either
totally frustrated or staring at the Beeb's Test Card. For ages.
(The Test Card then didn't have colour or the iconic image of

the girl with Bubbles the Clown, just lots of squares with a circle in the middle with more squares.)

Children's TV programming, such as *Andy Pandy*, *Whirligig*, *The Flowerpot Men* and *Watch with Mother* on the BBC, or ITV's *Noddy* (based on Enid Blyton's successful children's books) weren't likely to turn me into a tellyhog, partly because getting a picture could be a bit of a nightmare, but also because, by then, I had no truck with such kiddy stuff. (For all that, the *Noddy* characters, especially Big Ears and PC Plod, strode into everyday language: for decades afterwards, people would use those names to describe a nosy friend or a policeman.)

Books were my obsession: months after the coronation I headed for the bookshop opposite Princess May clutching my weekly two and sixpence pocket money, only to discover that the new picture book I really wanted to buy, the one with all the big black and white photos of the coronation, the ladies in waiting in their gorgeous white gowns, the cute little Prince Charles and Princess Anne watching their mum take on her awesome role, would cost more than I had. More pocket money, Dad? No problem. Those royal picture books were far more satisfying to me than the telly.

At one point, I bought a bestselling book called *The Little Princesses*. It was written, with the help of a ghostwriter, by a woman called Marion Crawford, who had been governess to the Princesses Elizabeth and Margaret when they were small. 'Crawfie', as they called her, revealed all sorts of very minor but fascinating things about the lives of the little princesses. Like the description Princess Margaret gave to a nursery meal of chopped-up meat, potatoes and gravy, calling it 'hoosh mi'.

Innocent trivia, yes. Not exactly the sort of thing to bring down the House of Windsor. But for those times, when deference still ruled and everyone worshipped the royals, even reading about royal nursery language was quite sensational.

Crawfie had retired in 1948, not long after the wedding of Elizabeth and Philip, when she finally got married herself after delaying her own marriage for sixteen years. Until the book came out, the royals had maintained warmly cordial relations with the former governess. But all communication ended abruptly with the publication of the book and Crawfie's own column in *Woman's Own* magazine. The royals never spoke to her again. And, yes, Crawfie was heartbroken.

Our TV, when it first arrived, couldn't offer anything quite as fascinating as a personal insight into the royals. A lot of the time what we got was just frustratingly fuzzy. Fiddle, fiddle, fiddle with the little indoor aerial for ages to just about get a picture, then watch the awful horizontal lines appear, irritatingly, right across the screen.

Since neither parent had any technical expertise whatsoever, this meant our early TV days weren't exactly as advertised, a cosy picture of smiling Mum and Dad plus happy children, enthralled as they stare at the magic box. More like frowning child hovering nervously while edgy or hung-over Dad fiddled with the aerial for a bit, then gave up and stomped off into the bedroom, only for Mum to come out of the kitchen to try fiddling to placate increasingly upset child who couldn't cope with the fact that it wouldn't work. If anything, that early TV was a source of rows and tantrums rather than undiminished pleasure.

Our big brown Bakelite radio, however, was not immediately replaced in our affections. It had played a hugely educational role during my very earliest years (when I'd recite, by rote, the BBC Shipping Forecast) and it wasn't likely to be banished nor ignored when the fuzzy TV arrived, since TV didn't really take over British life until the mid-1960s.

Shows on the Beeb's Light Programme like the wartime-themed *Much-Binding-in-the-Marsh* (tiddly om pom pom), *Educating Archie* (ventriloquist Peter Brough and his doll, a cute youthful Archie Andrews who at one stage was the country's most loved schoolboy: the show graduated to TV and remained popular for twenty years) and Sunday's *Billy Cotton Band Show* (Wakey-wakeee!) remain fixed powerful memories for millions.

Yet even in its infancy and fuzzy state, TV drama had the power to make inroads into my childish imagination, which already tended to be drawn to the extremes of dramatic shock horror rather than everyday programmes like the cute *Muffin the Mule*, the hugely popular puppet show presented by Annette Mills (sister of famed actor John Mills), which started on the BBC in 1952 and eventually moved to ITV.

I was enthralled by *The Quatermass Experiment*, an horrific early attempt in the summer of 1953 to scare the new TV audience stiff. The story is classic sci-fi, but it was pretty sensational for early TV: a rocket containing three men, the first humans ever to attempt space travel, crash lands – with only one crewman appearing to have survived. In fact, the trio are evolving into monstrous aliens – and humanity itself is imperilled. Strong stuff.

Even stronger – and equally enthralling to me, if quite scary – was the BBC TV adaptation of George Orwell's famous peek into a totalitarian future, *Nineteen Eighty-Four*, which was shown in December 1954.

The Beeb got a lot of flak for this. People were horrified – especially the Room 101 scene where Winston Smith was tortured by rats – and there was a newspaper story that a woman was so shocked when watching it, she collapsed and died.

Nonetheless, despite the controversy, the Beeb repeated it a week later – and got seven million viewers, the biggest TV audience since the coronation. At home, we watched the Sunday night repeat version – and Ginger, who hated rats, stormed out of the living room at the notorious scene. Today, of course, 'Room 101' represents a hilarious BBC TV comedy show.

But if the telly was still very much in its early days, the new G Plan style furniture that Molly acquired on HP from Davant's in our high street would become the permanent focal point of our small living room for decades, purchased to accompany the three-piece moquette lounge suite priced at an exorbitant £40, also on the never-never.

That plain teak extendable dining table, complete with four teak chairs with black vinyl seats, was where we sat down to eat all our meals, though there was rarely a time when we all ate together, such was my dad's bookie schedule.

Ginger rarely arrived home at a set time for an evening meal: he'd eat quite a lot of his meals in the Lane, often at a busy café directly opposite the Harrow Place office.

This café was run by a long-time pal of my dad's called Len, a man of Italian origin who could match my dad, joke for joke, for lively banter. They were great pals and would socialise frequently with their respective wives. So it was Len-from-the-caff who would frequently provide my dad's sustenance during the daytime hours, if he felt peckish, though it was more of the sausage, egg and chips (price: 1/6 for a full plateful) or sixpenny cheese roll variety rather than the spag bol or minestrone you'd associate with an Italian café now.

British food tastes then, even in the Lane with its cultural pot-pourri, were solidly of the meat-and-two-veg, egg-and-chips, jellied-eels, fish-and-chip variety. Tandoori chicken was a long way away.

'Foreign food? It's all muck,' Ginger would declare when I eagerly started to venture into Chinese-restaurant territory later on, after my working life started in the West End. 'Cat food, I betcha,' he'd snap, having always demonstrated a passionate aversion to Chinese or Japanese people. (Indians were okay because he'd been there in the war.)

Back then I'd decided my dad was a bigoted fool.

Now, on reflection, I realise he might have had a point... wherever you were, food hygiene standards in restaurants and cafés in the Fifties were not anything to write home about.

Pub food mostly consisted of the white-bread cheese sarnie. Even a Scotch egg, perched on a dusty plate in a smoke-filled bar, needed to be approached with caution. There was no 'elf and safety to keep regular tabs on catering standards. A girl in my class at Princess May once told Miss Budd, our teacher, that her mum had bought a 'fresh' loaf in Ridley Road only to discover a mouse baked inside it. We sat at our desks, stifling our glee, but once in the playground, we all ran around, shrieking with laughter. Mouse sandwich!

Many people couldn't yet afford to eat out in restaurants anyway, although that too would start to change a bit by the end of the decade. At home, many families adhered, pretty much, to a routine menu once rationing ended: a roast joint of meat with Yorkshire on Sunday (chicken was often too expensive and more likely served up as a treat at Christmas), cold leftover roast meat on Mondays with Crosse & Blackwell Branston Pickle, followed through the week by traditional Brit dishes like sausage and mash, shepherd's pie, meat stew with dumplings. Tinned meats like Spam or Fray Bentos corned beef were frequently served up – with lots of white bread and butter. Desserts were spotted dick or jam roly-poly with custard. Or stewed fruit accompanied by Carnation evaporated milk.

Food shopping was solidly local – high street butchers, fishmongers, fruit and veg, sweet shops. Or there were the abundant and busy street markets around where we lived, many still thriving today.

Ridley Road was the closest, so Molly went there mostly for fruit and veg. Her favourite stall was run by Becky, a very busty woman with a huge shock of upswept white blonde hair selling a wide range of women's underwear, especially knickers, brassieres and stockings, and everything at knockdown prices.

Molly, of course, an underwear saleslady herself through the war, loved to trade gossip with the boisterous, tireless Becky, who would expertly juggle the customers crowding her large stall at the top of the market – taking the fast-flowing cash, handing over change, swiftly wrapping three pairs of camiknickers and extolling the virtues of a pink full-length nylon slip as her customers fingered it – 'lovely, innit, you can 'ave two for five bob' – and diving below the stall's frontage to search for the right size.

As a schoolgirl, I was no longer required to accompany Molly on her trips to see Becky. I was immensely pleased about this because I had a permanent fear and loathing of Becky's husband, Vic, an immense bear of a man with a moustache, usually clad in a dark, three-piece suit, complete with waistcoat and fob watch. Vic ran other stalls, one in the Lane, so he wasn't around often. Yet he successfully damaged my equilibrium badly as a toddler and I never quite forgot it.

What did he do? One day, out of the blue, he just came around the counter and scooped me up, hitching me onto his shoulders, ready to parade me down Ridley Road. Terrified at this stranger's touch, I started screaming my head off. I wasn't an affectionate, cuddly kid anyway. To me this was sheer outrage.

'Blimey, Molly, your little Jacky's a terror,' Vic told my mum, depositing me back, still screaming, onto the ground by my mum's side. Terror Child, the pocket-sized air-raid siren, screamed at the top of her voice all the way back home.

A great deal of Vic and Becky's stock was 'nicked off the back of the lorry' stuff, but who cared, Becky's main competition (for those unwilling to risk anything dodgy) came from a big department store on the Kingsland Road, opposite Shacklewell Lane, called Dudley's.

Even now, the word Dudley's conjures up one vivid image:

a single shapely leg, encased in nylon, held aloft in the air, a Dudley's shop window dummy for Ballito stockings (seamless or fully fashioned, modom?), a hugely popular Fifties brand. Inside the store, like many other big shops then, they used an overhead wire-and-pulley arrangement on a pneumatic tube system, sometimes called a Lamson Paragon or Rapid Wire system, to take payment and send back change and the receipt.

The shop assistant would take your money, write out an invoice by hand and place that and the cash into a little rubber tube. This was whizzed across the ceiling via a system of wires and pulleys, or through the building via a pneumatic tube, to an accounts woman who sat in an office above the shop floor. She would then place the change and receipt back into the tube and whizz it back to the shop floor. It was cash only, no other means of payment in those days.

Stockings, of course (or nylons as they were called), complete with suspender belt or corset to hold them up, could also now be found at knockdown prices on market stalls. (During the war, nylon itself was needed for the war effort, so nylons became scarce and costly, with enterprising women simulating the seam of their 'stockings' by drawing a line down the back of their legs with black crayon, since the real thing was so difficult to source.) By the end of the Fifties, hosiery technology was changing women's lives with the onset of the new stretchy Lycra – and saw the beginning of tights, rather than stockings, in the Sixties.

We had plenty of other big street markets within a couple of miles, especially the very big one at Chatsworth Road (known locally as 'Chats'), which Molly knew well from living nearby in Oldhill Street, near Springfield Park, before she married Ginger.

Chats, she would often tell me, was huge: fish and shellfish stalls selling crab, winkles, whelks, mussels, shrimps, all measured out in little metal mugs. Live eels from The Eel Lady. A Home & Colonial store for groceries and a chemist's shop that sold a funny-sounding drink called sarsaparilla from a barrel outside the shop. (Sarsaparilla is made from the root of the sarsaparilla plant, mixed with sugar, water, liquorice and ginger. It was often served in pie-and-mash shops around the East End, though it was never served in our own local pie and mash shop in Dalston, Cooke's, which eventually closed its doors for good in 1997.)

'Much nicer than Ridley,' Molly would often sigh when reminiscing about Chats, though the nostalgia was probably more about her freedom years as a young single woman BG (Before Ginge).

A bit closer to us there was the Waste of Dalston, a street market which ran along the side of Kingsland High Street, specialising in – well, the name says it all – spare parts, old tools and rusty gardening equipment, although fruit and veg stalls also ran down the Waste, which positively thrived through the austerity of the early decade. There was also the Broadway Market further down around London Fields. Chapel Street market too was popular for fruit 'n' veg in nearby Islington, a ten-minute bus ride from Dalston, but back then, when such shopping sorties were usually conducted by women on foot, people stuck to their nearest market.

However, by then the supermarket was beginning, very slowly, to creep into British life: Tesco had opened Britain's very first self-service store in St Albans in 1947 and Sainsbury's opened their first purpose-built supermarket in Eastbourne in 1952. The only big local store brand recognisable locally today was our Sainsbury's at Dalston Junction, memorable for its unwrapped mounds of yellow butter served with a special butter pat or huge slabs of cheese, complete with cheese wire for slicing. (For many years I thought all cheese was Cheddar.) Everything seemed to come hand-wrapped in greaseproof paper or in a small brown paper bag; very little food was pre-wrapped or pre-packaged the way it is now.

The food we ate at home was a combination of the traditional meat 'n' two veg style and the Jewish dishes my mum had learned to cook from childhood. One of my dad's runners would deliver huge carrier bags of fresh fish from the Petticoat Lane stalls on a Friday, ready for my mum to fry in matzo meal or mince up to make gefilte fish (a traditional Jewish recipe made up of minced white fish with onion and carrot) using a tiny hand-operated metal mincer, complete with skinny handle. Salmon, haddock, plaice, prawns in their shells (in summer), smoked salmon, chickens to roast or make noodle soup, big joints of beef or legs of lamb to roast all made their way into the poky little kitchen. Plus offal, strangely enough.

Offal wasn't rationed during wartime, so it had always been plentiful. We'd have liver, usually cooked in the oven, and an odd but very tasty dish of stuffed hearts, tied up with string, that my mum would produce to go alongside the dishes of rice baked in the oven with sliced potatoes on top. Often, Ginger would come home late and eat cold whatever my mum had cooked for us that night.

But while she had, mostly, what she wanted my mum never cared much for the items that liberated so many women from slog. Our not-very-efficient Ewbank carpet sweeper, for instance, had been acquired for use, mostly by Annie, because we'd acquired a new green 'fitted' carpet (it wasn't fitted properly because, yet again, we'd sourced the services of an elderly local handyman, who was out of his depth with such modernity). In fact, the carpet sweeper only finally got chucked out nearly half a century later, alongside the small nest of three little teak tables in the living room, also a 1950s purchase from Davants, when Molly finally moved from the flat.

Only recently, I found an echo of these times, a Ridley Road shopping list in my mum's handwriting, written on the back of an old photo taken around 1948. I have no idea if it was written at that time – the bundles of wood suggest it might have been, as we still had coal fires right into the mid-1950s – but here it is:

Half a pound of butter
1 packet of cream crackers
4 bundles wood
Lyons cherry cake
10lb potatoes
1lb onions
1 packet of Daz (small)
1 packet of matzo meal (meal made from ground matzos, the unleavened bread traditionally eaten by Jewish people).

Lyons, of course, was a huge food brand then. Famous for their branded J. Lyons tea, cakes, biscuits and the big Lyons teashops with the white and gold fascia, Molly and I would sometimes pop into the Dalston Junction J. Lyons where my mum could get a decent cuppa for two and a half old pennies and, once food restrictions had ended, I'd happily tuck into a Knickerbocker Glory, a huge gooey confection of ice cream, cream, tinned fruit and cherries.

The four big multi-storied Lyons Corner Houses in London's West End were immensely popular during and beyond the Second World War. In fact, it was J. Lyons & Co who introduced the one food item that would spearhead all the big changes in Britain's food habits: the Wimpy, an American burger brand, launched under licence to J. Lyons as a speciality in 1954 at the Coventry Street Corner House; it was the country's first ever taste of the 'pure beef hamburger' (complete with tomato sauce from the red plastic squeezy container), priced at 2/-.

Initially, J. Lyons had been reluctant to go into the American idea of the fast-food market, believing that Brits weren't ready for it in 1950. Yet once it was launched, of course, the Wimpy took off with astonishing speed. Accompanied, if you fancied it, by a Whippsy (a thick ice cold milk shake) at 2/3, less than 5 bob for an outing or a treat – US-style eating, nigh on revolutionary for Blighty.

Very soon, high streets across Britain would be starting to sprout hundreds of Wimpy Bars. In a sense, those J. Lyons teashops, loved by all, were the McDonald's of their era, in that they catered to huge numbers, especially in wartime. Sadly, J.

Lyons teashops had vanished from high streets by 1998, joining many other high-street brands from the pre- and post-war era such as the Home & Colonial grocery chain, Black & White milk bars, Express Dairies, Mac Fisheries, Timothy Whites & Taylors (the chemists), ABC teashops, brands that had dominated so many high streets and lives for so long.

Local cinemas, of course, played a significant part in everyone's lives then, too. Cinema audiences were still huge in the 1950s and only really started to decline once TV really got into its stride in the 1960s.

We had a big ABC Cinema on the Kingsland Road, just a few minutes away. Saturday-morning pictures for kids were a highlight of the week. For sixpence you got two hours entertainment, cartoons, a feature film and sometimes an episode of a serial like *Jungle Girl* or *Batman*. Some of the films were Westerns starring Roy Rogers, Gene Autry or the legendary Hopalong Cassidy. The programme always started with the kids' own song, the 'ABC Minors Song', with the words coming up on the screen, accompanied by a bouncy ball.

> We are the boys and girls known as
> Minors of the ABC
> And every Saturday we line up
> To see the films we like
> And shout about with glee
> We like to laugh and have a singsong
> Such a happy crowd are we
> We're all pals together
> We're Minors of the ABC.

I went along with my friend from Princess May, Sandra Holland, a quiet sort of girl with long dark hair. She'd been going to Saturday-morning pictures for ages and loved it. I dropped out after a few times. It was a bit rowdy and, if truth be told, I preferred my books to a noisy cinema full of screaming kids. Nor was I mad about Westerns or cartoons.

Weekly magazines aimed at girls my age, like *Girl*, price four and a half pennies, launched in 1951 as a 'sister' publication to the popular boy's comic *Eagle*, didn't hold my attention for long. The magazine had a comic-strip format, with the story told in drawings with speech bubbles. I preferred solid text, page after page. I wasn't a regular cinema goer until into my late teens – and then it was mostly for foreign movies because I was so influenced by French and Italian culture. The Classic Continental on Kingsland High Street, an art deco cinema built in the Thirties, was destined to become an art or foreign movie house much later on. But by then, I'd left the area.

One day, I arrive home from school to find Molly chatting on the phone to an old wartime friend called Bessie. They'd lost touch but they'd recently bumped into each other in Ridley Road, where Bessie was hunting down some fabric. Bessie is a milliner, quite a few years older than Molly; in wartime she'd worked briefly with my mum before being evacuated to Wales with her small daughter, Marion.

I'd heard about Bessie before: my mum had often reminisced about Bessie's love of hats and her earthy, no nonsense ways – 'I narf cleaned her' was her favourite phrase, my mum told me (translation: Bessie told a woman off, in no uncertain terms).

Now Bessie is insisting Molly come round for a cup of tea the following Saturday, a reunion Molly welcomed. The Bessie family now lived in a house in Clapton, not that far away and a bit of a trip down memory lane for my mum.

'I'm not telling your dad, Jac, but I'm definitely going. She wants you to come with me. She's got a boy now, too; he's your age. Her husband won't be there. Saturdays he goes to a garage in Clapton Pond with his mates so they can muck about with their motorbikes.'

'Do I have to go, mum?' I grumble, having never looked too closely at any motorbike, though sales of motorcycles soared through the Fifties and by the end of the decade nearly 250,000 bikes were registered – a golden age of the motorbike, complete with the all-important sidecar attached, so the family could travel, too.

I am reluctant because I know my mum just wants to gossip with Bessie, talk about the old times. Sometimes war talk was interesting – the younger me had been fascinated by my dad's journey to far-off India – but by now, at home, I've heard enough about the war.

I'd been told all about Hitler, how he would have murdered us, as Jews, if Churchill hadn't saved the day. I'd seen the scary photos of the concentration camps with the piles of corpses in my dad's paperback books, heard him repeat, time and again, that we had to drop the H-bomb on the Japanese because 'you couldn't beat 'em', and had frequently heard my mum's story about the day she turned up to work in Oxford Street during the Blitz, only to find her workplace a smouldering ruin. War, war – that was all the adults seemed to go on about. Jack and Miriam too could dish out their fair share of war chat. Enough.

'Look, Jac, it's only for a couple of hours,' pleads my mum. 'She asked specially for you to come too. It'll look bad for me if you don't.'

And so I go. It's such a rare kind of outing, I'm half intrigued. That day, my mum and I, both togged up nicely, Molly in her big circular black and white skirt with white cap-sleeved blouse, me in a little white Aertex cotton top and dirndl skirt, make the journey by bus and long walk to Blurton Street, where the Bessie family live in a big four-storey terraced house. We've had a couple of outings to visit Evelyn in the suburbs, but this is first time we've visited anyone in the area around us, other than my grandparents. So today is something different.

'They live in the basement and the first floor and they let the second floor to lodgers,' Molly tells me as we make our way there. Her Dave's self-employed, like Ginge, but he's a builder. They have to have the lodgers because he couldn't get any work after the war.'

So bad was it, my mum said, that Bessie had to 'take in' ironing for a long time. 'But now Dave's starting to get work again.'

At the front door Bessie greets us. She's in her mid-forties, fair-haired, wearing a grey pencil skirt with a wide belt and a short-sleeved pale yellow blouse. Like my mum, she's got full warpaint on, foundation, red lipstick, blue eyeshadow, lots of powder. Perched on her head is a small dark 'pancake' hat, a tribute to her former life as a milliner.

To me, the house seems enormous. We're ushered into a big front room and it's really quite impressive, newly decorated with a plain rust-coloured fitted carpet and a green three-piece moquette suite, quite similar to our new suite. The ceilings are very high too, unlike our low-ceilinged habitat.

There's a big new fireplace surrounded by a mock drystone wall and in the centre, a built-in Berry's Magicoal, one of the new electric fires I'd seen advertised in the papers, priced at £21 3s 2d. Magicoals looked just like a coal fire, but all you needed to do was flick a switch to turn them on and heat the room.

Bessie sees me peering at it.

'Like it, Jacky? My Dave built that. Heats the place up a treat. You gonna get one, Molly?'

'No, Ginge says we're better off with a new gas fire from the Gas Board,' my mum says flatly. She doesn't seem as impressed as I am by the Magicoal.

I'd overheard a conversation about heating after my mum had showed Ginger an ad in the paper for a new Aladdin paraffin heater – 'in every room' the ad said.

'Nah, Mol,' my dad said. 'Too much muckin' abaht, fillin' em.'

Which just about summed up my dad's attitude. Just take the easiest option was his mantra. All over the country, men like Bessie's Dave had used their practical DIY skills to help get their family through the lean years and now, with prosperity looming, they were busy building new things for their home, getting out and about with their families, maybe buying one of the new Morris Minor cars or, like Dave, lovingly tending to a new Royal Enfield motorbike, which would also give the family the freedom of the road.

My dad just followed in Jack's footsteps at work and play. Cabs and buses were easy. Who needed to drive? Hire a big posh car to take you to seaside holidays. There was a taxi rank, complete with phone, at Dalston Junction, so some mornings, my dad would walk down there and cab it to work and the Lane. His brother, Ginger No. 2, was starting to focus on suburban family life, made easier by the purchase of a new Ford Anglia. But Ginger didn't care to consider driving: there was always cash for someone to drive you around, wasn't there?

Bessie briefly disappears into the basement scullery to get our tea.

When she comes back, bearing a huge tray laden with perfectly cut-up sandwiches, cakes and biscuits, there's a boy behind her, also carrying a tray with plates, cups and saucers and the teapot, which are all carefully placed on a nearby side table.

Today's a bit of a feast. What they used to call a High Tea. There's a choice of sandwiches: cheese and pickle, luncheon meat and tomato, fish paste, as well as a Lyons cream sponge cake, already cut up, and a big plate of biscuits: Bourbon, Nice, Peek Freans, choccy digestives.

'That's our David,' says his mum, who has now removed her hat. We mutter our hellos. David's fair, just like his mum, blue eyes, grey short trousers, sandals with socks, and a short-sleeve check shirt. He looks quite pleasant. Definitely not a scruff. Or a ruffian. No spots, anyway.

Molly and I sit in the armchairs, David goes downstairs again to bring up a bottle of Tizer ('the Appetiser') and two glasses for our refreshment. He pours one glass, carefully hands it to me, then sits down next to his mum on the sofa after pouring himself a glass.

'Thanks,' I say, but I'm far too unused to boys to venture further, so I eagerly sip the red fizzy liquid. David too remains quiet, but more polite than sullen. That was how it was then. Eleven-year-olds in the company of adults, especially strangers, weren't expected to chat easily to everyone.

'Our David's a clever sod,' says his mum, proudly, offering Molly and me a small selection of sandwiches. Soon, I'm tucking into a fish-paste sarnie, something we don't have at home. (I did wonder why Bessie didn't offer Crosse & Blackwell sandwich spread, like at home, but thought it best to keep quiet.)

'Passed that eleven-plus, didn't you, David?'

'Yeah but I don't know which school yet... ' ventures Clever Sod David, whose mum promptly talks right over him.

'We think either that Grocers' Company School or the Owen's in Islington – but Dave and me thinks it don't matter, they're all the same. And the uniforms! So bloody expensive!'

'Jac's passed hers, too,' says my mum.

'Did you think it was easy?' David asks me, somewhat surprisingly.

Hmm. Yes, it wasn't as bad as they all kept saying,' I tell him, half turning but not really looking at Clever Sod.

I'm far too embarrassed to say any more, even though I knew the Grocers' school, officially known as the Hackney Downs

School, was quite close by. You saw boys wearing the uniform – a blue blazer with a school badge – often enough around Dalston.

'Mmm. These sandwiches are nice, did you get the tomatoes at Chats?' Molly queries.

'Oh that's our Dave, grows 'em in our garden. You should see 'im, Molly. Whenever the rag-and-bone man comes down 'ere, Dave's running outside wavin' 'is pan and brush to collect the 'orse dung for 'is tomatoes.'

Molly's a bit stunned at this. She doesn't quite choke on her sandwich but it's close. I'm shocked too. We are not horticulturalists, my mum and I. We don't know that something as smelly as horse manure – occasionally found in steaming piles on Dalston's roads back then – can be deployed as fertiliser to produce tasty tomatoes.

'Bit of a gardener, is he?' Molly says, recovering quickly.

'Yeah, got 'is vegetable patch. But that bike is the thing 'e really loves. Your Ginge got one, Mol?'

'Er no, Ginger loves sport, the gee-gees and the football,' Molly explains.

'Ah. Well, we used ter like the bike, didn't we David? When 'e was small, on Sundays we'd go out to the country, me ridin' pillion, David standin' up in the sidecar shoutin', "Faster, daddy, faster".'

'Too big for all that now, eh?'

The women smile at each other, the complicit look of 'well, they're growing up now, our kids'. David finishes his Tizer, carefully places the glass on the table and says, 'Just going out to the garden, Mum, bye Jacky, bye Molly,' and departs.

'Nice and big, this house,' Molly says, looking round the room. 'Reminds me of where we lived when I was a kid.'

'Yeah, it's big enough for Marion and her 'usband to stay 'ere, up on the top floor. They're savin' up now for a place of their own. Used to be a real posh 'ouse in its day. Doctor lived 'ere. Must've 'ad lots of servants. Still got the servants' bells on the wall down there.'

Then, of course, it's gossip time over the cake and cuppas. I'm happy: Bessie leaps up to ensure there's another slice of cream sponge in front of me.

Mostly, the two women trade stories about their respective neighbours, Molly's ongoing silent war with the detested Maisie, the ground-floor harridan in our block. Maisie has always resented our well-shod presence in what is, essentially, an environment where we look distinctly out of place.

'That son of hers, Bessie, he STINKS, doesn't he, Jac?'

I nod, wondering if I'll get told off for requesting a third slice of cream sponge, but then decide against it. I've remembered there's a Lyons sponge cake in the new fridge at home.

'Well, we've got our share 'ere.'

'We 'ad that Fanny Fink and 'er girl livin' 'ere as lodgers, till they moved down the road. Terrible, they was. Everyone knew the girl 'ad no dad, cos of the war and the filth.' ('Filth', I would discover a long time later, was often used by women as a euphemism for sex.)

'And as for that Tiny next door and 'er kids... disgustin'. Everyone calls 'er Nitty Norah.'

And so the afternoon rolls on, the women reminiscing – not

too much war this time – trading bits of information about their lives, their spouses.

As for their two clever eleven-plus kids, I never meet David or Bessie again, and while Molly keeps up the friendship by phone for some time, she doesn't return the invite: too much hassle with Ginger.

Many years later, Molly ran into Bessie in Ridley. David, it turned out, went to Owen's (Dame Alice Owen's School, to give it the correct name, now an academy located in Potters Bar). He stopped studying after a couple of years and became a bit of a teen rebel. Later, he wound up at art school. Then, much to Bessie's amazement, at age twenty-two he announced that he was emigrating to Australia. Ten pounds for a new life. In the Fifties and Sixties more than a million migrants from Britain emigrated to Australia under what was known as the Assisted Passage Migration Scheme, created after the Second World War to increase the Australian population and provide workers for the country. The fare was £10 (children travelled free) and families were obliged to stay for two years.

'We don't think our Dave'll ever come back,' Bessie told Molly wistfully. Back then, in the pre-jumbo jet era, a new life in Oz often meant families believed they were unlikely to see the émigrés again.

David, Molly heard from his mum afterwards, did return. He came nearly every year at one stage for holidays. Nevertheless, the move from Hackney proved to be a permanent one...

CHAPTER 4

SET ON THE CREST OF A BUSY HILL

Not long after the Bessie's visit, a decision was needed. City of London wasn't interested, so which grammar school would I go to?

There had been three choices in the letter informing us I'd passed: Dalston County (literally a few minutes' walk around the corner from us in Shacklewell Lane), Laura Place (or the John Howard Grammar School for Girls, to give it its correct title) in Lower Clapton, and The Skinners' Company School for Girls up in Stamford Hill.

Wherever I went, it meant buying brand new school uniforms. I wasn't initially keen on this. Nor were a few other families in the area – because they were frequently counting every penny. Some families, just like Bessie's, viewed the cost of grammar-school uniforms – which we were informed could only be purchased from specific school outfitters in posh locations – as a cost too far.

In a way, this was a case of middle-class values being imposed on ordinary working-class people who were frequently struggling, post-war, with the weekly bills. To them, another £40–£50 or thereabouts towards their child's future was a considerable strain on the family's budget. Additionally, these special grammar-school uniforms would easily set us apart from our local peer group. In down-at-heel Hackney we grammar-school first-years would be automatically labelled stuck-up or snobbish. The epithet 'Skinners' School for Snobs' followed me through my time there.

In a few cases, it wasn't just the cost of uniforms: parents of really bright kids who were offered scholarships to ultra-prestigious schools were also expected to contribute a nominal amount towards school fees.

This, I knew, had happened to Sandra Holland's family when an older brother had been awarded a place at a prestigious boarding school outside London. With three children and one office worker's wage coming in, plus Sandra's mum's part-time wages from a local canteen, times remained tight for the Hollands. They just couldn't manage an ongoing fee each term. So her brother wound up at a local grammar.

'Mum says it was lucky they had a bit put by it in the Post Office, otherwise they couldn't've even paid for the uniform,' Sandra confided.

At the time, I didn't ask Sandra why her dad 'put it in the Post Office', simply because the concept of saving money for a rainy day never came up in conversation at home. I didn't even know about piggy banks, frequently used to encourage a savings habit in kids.

I'd more or less absorbed the belief that money bought you whatever you wanted – and it was readily available. Mind you, it had confused me on one of our visits to 'the buildings' when I heard grandmother Miriam tell Molly to make sure she went through my dad's pockets when he was asleep and take whatever she wanted.

Why would she do that? I thought. My dad was always handing my mum money, I saw that all the time. I didn't understand that Miriam's rationale was that any money she herself nicked was money that wouldn't be spent in the pub, so Molly should follow suit.

If I asked my dad for money, he just handed me some silver, first a shilling, later half a crown when I was old enough to run down the road to buy my own sweets or books. If he wasn't around, I'd get my mum to open her purse for what I wanted. Neither parent ever led me to believe that there wasn't an unending pile of coins and notes available at any time. I knew my dad liked the new HP – but that kind of made sense. Have it now, pay later. Sounded good to me.

In the end, of course, The Old Man held sway with the decision on my future. Molly and Ginger knew that had I won that prized City of London scholarship, The Old Man would have generously offered to pay any tuition fees, a whopping £70 a term at the time. So his was the final say.

'He thinks Jacky's better off at Skinners',' Ginger reported back to us. 'It's a London Livery company: you used to have to pay to go there when he was young. It's got a very good reputation.'

My dad was right. The Worshipful Company of Skinners was one of the Great Twelve Livery companies of the City of London. It dates right back to medieval times when it was the trade guild of furriers. Today, The Skinners' Company is a major not-for-profit organisation involved in running schools, sheltered housing, educational institutions and a wide range of small organisations throughout the UK (the Stamford Hill school eventually became a comprehensive girls' school and in recent years evolved into the Skinners' Academy, based in nearby Woodberry Down.)

Perhaps the story might have been different had I insisted I wanted to go to one of the other schools.

But neither of my primary-school friends, Sandra Holland and Kathy Shilling, had got top marks in the eleven-plus. They'd be going to the newly opened Woodberry Down, secondary modern at Manor House, a new building and a huge enterprise in the late Fifties, with some 1,400 pupils. So I'd be on my own wherever I went.

By then, however, I had discovered something important: the Skinners' school uniform was much envied in the area – mostly because of the outstandingly stylish and distinctive red-and-black-striped Skinners' blazer. Laura Place girls had a raw deal: their uniforms consisted of a brown tunic, yellow blouse, brown blazer – and brown knickers, a horrific idea for any girl. So Skinners' definitely had clothing cachet. An easy journey too:

just a 243 bus ride from outside Princess May up to Stamford Hill, journey time fifteen to twenty minutes. Decision made.

'We have to go to a place called Kinch & Lack in Victoria, Mum, to get the uniforms,' I tell Molly, excitedly, re-reading the printed letter we'd received about Skinners' uniforms.

So off we go, Molly as proud as punch with a big bundle of Ginger's fivers in her bag (there were no £10, £20 or £50 notes back then) sitting on the top deck of the 38 bus from Dalston Junction to Victoria in her new expensive beige Alligator raincoat with huge buttons on the cuffs and at the front. Super-smart.

She'd recently bought the coat at Marshall & Snelgrove, a really posh department store on Oxford Street. It was very big store, like many in the area, but Molly was familiar with the big department stores around the West End from her working days and would never be the least bit daunted by their size and somewhat grand surrounds (given the class-consciousness of the time, some assistants could be incredibly condescending towards anyone they felt didn't fit the upmarket profile of their store).

Effectively, my mum felt she was an 'insider', knew the retail ropes, as it were. She didn't have a 'Oh, I'm as good as you' stroppy attitude, nor was she deferential. She was just herself, smiley, warm and attractive. It worked a treat.

Shopping trips together, of course, had involved going to the West End long before this trip to Kinch & Lack in Artillery Row, just off Victoria Street. We'd often go up West to buy me new shoes: something quite exciting for kids in the early Fifties because many shoe shops proudly offered their customers a pedoscope.

This was, in fact, an X-ray machine promoted by shoe retailers as a way of making sure kids' shoes fitted properly. At one point, there were about 3,000 of these machines installed in shoe shops across the UK. There was a slot at the bottom of the machine for your feet, and you could stand on the machine and, through a hole at the top, peer in and see the skeleton of your feet in the new shoes you were trying on (in my case, usually 'Mary Jane' style with an inset strap).

Good fun for kids. Disastrous for tiny feet when the real hazards of these X-ray machines – interference with bone growth and skin damage – became known, and the pedoscopes vanished from shoe shops in the late Fifties.

Molly's easy manner certainly helps when an extremely snooty man at Kinch & Lack strides forward to greet us, giving us a very obvious once-over and sniffing quite visibly when Molly cheerfully explains how I've passed the eleven-plus and require a uniform. Then he somewhat grudgingly agrees to take our order, measure me up, as Molly watches, puffed up with pride and completely unfazed by this version of retail snobbery. Later on, I discovered that there was a similar posh school-uniform department store called Daniel Neal (in Kensington High Street). These stores usually treated their customers with respect and deference – provided they came from the right background.

Purchasing the Skinners' uniform takes ages because it involves so much: relevant detailed orders must be written down for the fine wool red and black striped blazer, grey Robert Hirst gabardine raincoat (never worn), grey woollen beret (ditto), grey

V-neck woollen jumper with thin red stripe around the V (perfect styling: I'd still be wearing one now if only I'd kept it) and grey woollen six-panel skirt (decent enough but ruined in the end, as I'd shove the contents of unwanted school dinners into a paper bag and leave it in the pocket for ages). Then there were the pink and white seersucker short-sleeved Skinners' blouses, pink-and-white-striped summer dresses, the red elasticated belt, the games kit of white Aertex short-sleeved top and very short skirt. Quite a big financial undertaking.

Families in Hackney who couldn't afford everything would, I found out later, simply improvise, buying certain items, like a grey skirt, for instance, from cheap chain stores like the now defunct C&A, ignoring the 'rules' – which didn't go down well at all with the teaching staff, leaving one or two new girls deeply embarrassed. But the one thing every family had to purchase was the blazer: it was a unique item. You couldn't fudge that.

At last, the list is completed. Yet the outlay does not quite end there.

'Will you be ordering the Cash's name tapes, modom?' says Mr Sniffy, probably thinking that Molly would recoil in horror at the extra expense. (The name tapes were specially made. Each individual name tape had to be cut from a long linen tape in order to be sewn onto individual garments. What a palaver.)

'Oh that's fine,' smiles Molly. 'Look, Jac, you'll have your name on everything!'

I'm pretty impressed with the idea of having my name printed on a tape (the ego had landed long ago). Ten out of ten for that idea.

'Can I have one of those name tapes now?' I ask Mr Sniffy, not realising that they come on one continuous tape.

He stares at me, this skinny man in his well-cut suit.

By now, he's noted our address, knows exactly which side of London's social divide we represent. To him, we belong with all the war-weary masses who'd huddled together to sleep on the packed Tube platforms during the bombings just over a decade back. Not quite respectable enough, by his standards.

East Enders coming in here, ordering expensive school uniforms? Just what was the world coming to?

'No, you can't. It's not possible,' he snaps, not bothering to explain

Only afterwards do we realise that the name tapes were not essential. (They were, of course, essential for boarding-school pupils, but those at day schools didn't have to have them for everything other than hats, raincoats or sports kit.) We could have easily said no. A bit of a rip-off really, though Molly didn't mind sewing each one onto each individual item: a labour of love.

At the time, the cost of all this, around £50, would have been equivalent to just over a month's wages for the average working person, a good example of the price of stepping up a notch, gaining social mobility.

Looking back, the eleven-plus exam was a social experiment set up by well-meaning politicians at a time when class still mattered very much in Britain. Why shouldn't they attempt to give all of us a chance? Given what had happened to people's lives during the war, families had certainly 'earned' the right to a better deal for their kids' education.

Did it work?

Many nowadays insist it was too divisive, a giant mistake. Yet for some Hackney kids the eleven-plus exam did eventually lead to university, even Oxbridge, Britain's turbo-charged ticket to opportunity. For me? In the few years I was at Skinners', I would acquire a certain amount of knowledge (so-so French in a reasonable accent, anyone?) plus an expensive, stylish blazer. Complete with unnecessary name tape.

I was more curious than wildly excited by all this change ahead. I took everything, including the pricey uniform, for granted, didn't believe I had to 'deliver' in any sense, unlike other kids I knew who understood all too well that their parents had been struggling for ages for every penny and they'd better not let them down.

'My mum won't answer the door if it's the insurance man,' Sandra Holland had told me one day in the playground at Princess May. 'She says it's Dad's fault because he took out the policy and we can't really afford it.'

Door-to-door insurance collectors (and salesmen) were a regular feature of everyday life then, as were landlords who would knock on the front door each week to collect the rent in person, noting everything down in the neat little rent book.

Most families, like the Hollands, kept Post Office accounts to 'put something by', but it was usually those running their own business who used bank accounts and cheque books as Ginger did. Post-dated cheques (cheques dated a month or even more ahead) were something he also used frequently.

However, the daily battle against poverty was all too common for those who didn't have any bank account or form of credit, other than buying 'on tick', which was an informal form of credit a shopkeeper would sometimes allow a customer. But if there was a man on the doorstep (and it was usually a man) wanting payment and there was no cash to hand over, on the spot, the only option was to be 'out'.

I knew so little beyond the horizons of my somewhat limited world: Kingsland Road to Liverpool Street and back, with seaside holidays each year to the Kent coast. I'd been up to the somewhat leafier streets of Stamford Hill a few times – Molly had sent me to a posh nursery (a kindergarten, as they called it then) there before grudgingly sending me to the primary school Urchins' Den of Colvestone Crescent – but that was the sum total of my geographic experience of the world around me, other than the odd trip to Evelyn's house in the far off 'burbs and what I read about in books or newspapers.

But what could the far-off fictional world of Enid Blyton's Malory Towers, a posh girls' boarding school in Cornwall, tell a Dalston bookie's daughter about the reality of joining a school like Skinners', whose teachers came from a rigid, class-bound Edwardian era where women had only been permitted to teach provided they remained single? (This too did not change until around the time of the new Education Act in 1944.)

Being Jewish, of course, was not unusual for the area around Stamford Hill, which encompassed Hackney, Clapton and Stoke Newington – indeed, Skinners' had such a high intake of Jewish girls – around one third of pupils were Jewish at that time – that due acknowledgement was made to our religious requirements and there were twice-weekly separate assemblies for Jewish girls.

There were also classes in religious instruction, ie learning Hebrew, though my year showed a quite shameful disrespect for Mr Dov, the man who came to teach us and spoke very oddly, his favourite phrase being, 'Come ye out.'

Ill-equipped to handle classes of noisy teenage girls, he had a rough time: at one point stink bombs were thrown in the classroom. It goes without saying that I didn't learn much Hebrew beyond a few letters of the alphabet.

For all that the school governors had taken their responsibilities to the local community very seriously, political correctness remained a distant dream in the Fifties. Our teachers, professional women, mostly unmarried – many had lost potential partners in the Great War – were mainly spinsterish, prim types. One or two could be quite chillingly forbidding. Our Latin teacher, Miss McLelland, clearly held us all in considerable disdain: she had an utterly disarming habit of addressing everyone as 'Creature'.

This stern, authoritarian style of teaching was, alas, somewhat in contrast to my primary-school experience. There the teachers had been mostly pleasant and enthusiastic about their young charges – despite having to teach large numbers of working-class kids, around forty to a class.

Skinners' curriculum was a combination of learning and sport, which included netball, hockey, gym and other athletic pursuits. If you were really good at sport, you were liked by the teachers, a favourite, even if you weren't much cop at study. I hated and shunned all forms of sport whenever possible, my excuses for non-participation becoming increasingly creative as time went on. So much love would never be lost between me and my teachers.

My arrival at grammar school in the autumn of 1956 also took place at a point in time where conflict between the generations was beginning, gradually, to emerge in ways not seen before on the street, giving the authorities a real wake-up call. With rebellion against my immediate environment already bubbling away, biding its time, I was bound to be influenced by the external forces, more than anything else. I stepped up to grammar school without any preconceived notions of possible achievement or any determined drive to succeed. There was never going to be any push from home to get my head down, to keep studying. For my parents, just seeing me dressed in that smart Skinners' uniform was reward enough.

In fact, on my very first day when I stepped through the big red front-door entrance to the school to gaze in awe at the imposing wood-panelled high-ceilinged assembly area, with its tall stained-glass windows, big clock and big organ, complete with pipes, I realised I was totally unprepared for this new setting and what it might entail. A new country, in uncharted territory called Discipline.

What I then learned about my new environment came as a huge shock to me. Not because I was going to be tackling brand-new subjects like French and Latin – French came relatively easy, Latin was ghastly and only to be appreciated when you no longer had to study it – but I had no idea until then that other girls around my age were already immersed in what I considered far-off, grown-up things.

Some of the girls in my year and above were from comfortably-off middle-class homes. They travelled abroad regularly with their families. Yet they weren't merely worldly travellers – they were already wearing bras, nylon stockings and talking about boyfriends. They had taken those first steps into the adult world. I hadn't even thought about going there. Yet.

When I look back at it all now, it was obvious I'd be intimidated by it all. Most of us were. The place itself was incredibly imposing, proud of its history, its traditions. 'To God only be all glory' was the motto of the Worshipful Company of Skinners.

Even more glory was underlined in the final chorus of the school song, 'Skinners', glorious Skinners". Yet what those initial weeks revealed to me, alongside the pomp of the school's proud status, was this: not only would I be sitting alongside girls who were just as bright as me, just as good as what I considered 'my' subjects (English and history, mostly), but some of these girls were quite 'fast', already doing adult things I'd never dreamed of. Precocious teens.

One girl, Enid, let it be known to all and sundry that she was practically engaged. I didn't need a brassiere then, but when we changed for gym class, it was clear that those that wore one definitely did. One or two were already carrying lipstick (I'd not really considered it, which was odd with Molly's daily make-up routines). But worst of all, for me, once the star turn on stage, I realised that a few girls in my year were astonishingly adept at something I couldn't do: jive to the new rock 'n' roll music.

I stood there at lunchtime, about a month after I started, as a nervous first year, alone in the large grassy area at the back of the main building, watching two girls from the year above, Pauline and Carole, practising their jiving technique. They were experts. Slick. It looked like they'd been doing it for years. Nowadays, they'd have been acclaimed as winners on *Strictly*.

I was horrified. I couldn't do that! I didn't even have anyone to practise with!

Jiving was not really new. Jitterbugging, quite similar to jiving but far more energetic, even acrobatic, had been the big thing in the States since the Thirties. Then the GIs came over here during the war and started showing off their version of it, dubbed jiving, on the dance floor. By the early Fifties, jiving youngsters were taking to the floor in dance halls and jazz clubs in droves – until the whole jiving thing literally exploded in Britain when Bill Haley appeared in the local cinema, complete with kiss-curl, in the movie *Blackboard Jungle*, playing 'Rock Around the Clock' in September 1956, the same month I started at Skinners'.

'One, two, three o clock, four o clock rock… ' Haley's beat was so infectious that at the cinema, the enthusiastic young audiences started clapping their hands, banging their feet until they just leaped out of their seats into the cinema aisles and started jiving to the new rock 'n' roll music. Somehow, it all got out of hand. The police were called. Scuffles with the police resulted in crowds of kids booing and yelling outside cinemas all over London. One song – and rock 'n' roll mania had landed in Britain.

The story of the jiving teens made headlines everywhere. Teddy boys were at the heart of the cinema mayhem, according to all the newspapers. By then, the 'Teds' were a uniquely Brit phenomenon, a cipher for rebellious youth, if you like: the country's first-ever teen tribe. Feared and hated in equal measure.

My dad would frequently bring home a weekly magazine called *Picture Post*, which featured all kinds of interesting news stories accompanied by compelling black and white photos. The Teddy boys with their Edwardian style, velvet-collared long draped jackets, longish greased-back hair with a quiff at the front and a DA (duck's arse) at the back featured prominently in the magazine.

Gangs of Teds with drainpipe trousers, narrow bootlace ties and an ever-present comb in their hand (they were always combing their long hair), plus thick crepe-soled suede 'brothel-creeper' footwear (as worn by British soldiers in North Africa who reputedly frequented brothels) had emerged on Britain's streets around 1953, much to the total bewilderment of the adult world. At a time when respectability was all, the Teds, with their reputation for violence, flick knives and gang fights, were seriously demonised.

I hadn't actually seen *Blackboard Jungle*, though of course, a few Teds could be spotted sometimes, hanging around the streets of Dalston. What had fascinated me, via the newspaper and magazine photos I'd seen even before the movie arrived, were the wide circular skirts (held out with nylon petticoats underneath) flying out around the girls as they jived: I'd always study newspaper photos for hints of what other girls were wearing.

At one point before Skinners' I'd nagged Molly and we did go out and buy a full patterned skirt for me to wear over a stiff petticoat, acquired from Dudley's, but I was not in the least influenced by the Teddy Girl fashions spotted in newspaper photos; these were copycat versions of the male Teddy style: waistcoats, tailored jackets with velvet collars, high-necked collars and flat berets with a pin with a pearl in them. You never saw a Teddy Girl around Dalston; there just weren't that many of them around.

Until then, fashion influences on youngsters came mostly from two different directions: the Teddy boy style that was heavily influenced by Edwardian menswear and the other influence, well established, from Hollywood and the movies, of course.

The full wide skirts, often accompanied by pony-tail hairdo, bobby socks and flat shoes, were very much style-setting fashions as seen in US movies like *Rock Around the Clock*, soon released to cash in on the success of Haley's appearance in *Blackboard Jungle*.

I was a bit too young for the movie actor James Dean cult – he'd died in a road accident in 1955 – but there's no question of the influence of Dean's 'look' from *Rebel Without a Cause*: to this day, the tight white T-shirt, black leather jacket, denim jeans and boots he wore remain an enduring classic style.

But what we weren't aware of then was that here in Britain, our home-grown fashion influencers, the Pied Pipers for millions of kids, were already setting up their stalls: Mary Quant's famous Bazaar shop had recently opened in Chelsea's King's Road in 1955 and very soon, in a tiny, unknown narrow street behind

Regent Street in the West End, a young Glaswegian called John Stephen was about to open his first menswear shop in Carnaby Street in 1957. This was a hugely successful enterprise, a fashion revolution in Mod clothing. Stephen later became known as The King of Carnaby Street, such was his influence.

In those first months at a new school, you're just working everything out, the teachers, the other girls, those you might want to be friends with – if they'd have you. Tight little cliques were already being established, but I didn't get involved in any friendships straight away. I was pretending indifference, hiding any shyness, a typical early teen, affecting sophistication where none existed, secretly planning my first expedition to Woolworths to purchase a pink lipstick with my pocket money (I didn't worry straight away about actually wearing it; I just had to have one).

Yet my fake cool was shattered one afternoon after leaving a French lesson. Pamela Edwards, a girl I hadn't really talked to before, accosted me in the long corridor: 'You're Jacky Hyams, the Sorcerer's Apprentice, aren't you?' she said, her yellow-blonde hair tied up in a bouncy pony-tail style that really suited her and made her stand out from the crowd.

'Yeah, how do you know that?' I asked.

'Oh my little sister Brenda's at Princess May. She wasn't in your year but me and my mum went to watch her in that concert you did at the Town Hall.'

It had been my last-ever star turn on the stage, as the Sorcerers' Apprentice, just weeks before at Stoke Newington Town Hall. A few other kids from Princess May had been in it, but Pamela

Edwards's sister didn't ring any bells, probably because I never spoke to any of the younger girls.

'Don't know your sister, sorry.'

'No, but everyone said it was your dad, wasn't it, that was making all the racket after it finished, when everyone was singing "God Save the Queen"?'

Oh no. Please don't remind me of my shame.

Ginger had insisted on coming to the concert late, after work. I'd been praying he somehow wouldn't turn up because I knew he'd be three sheets to the wind, as he was most nights.

But he came in late and perched himself right at the back towards the end. And, sure enough, he did his usual boozy trick, joining in the national anthem at the very top of his voice. (It was traditional then at the end of any concert, theatre or cinema performance for the audience to stand to attention and sing the national anthem, an act of deference that finally ended during the Sixties.)

Of course the assembled parents and siblings had noticed and looked askance at the well-dressed, stout, red-faced man practically yodelling 'SEND 'ER VICTORIOUS, 'APPY AND GLORIOUS', giving it considerable welly. No one in the place could miss it.

Molly, further forward in the audience, said nothing afterwards. At times like these, she'd just blank it all out. She preferred to cover herself in my glory up there on the stage, the mum of the apprentice, the youth with the axe. As we took our bows, hearing him whistling his piercing whistle amidst the enthusiastic applause, I just about managed to conceal my tears – and my anger. Why did he have to go and spoil everything?

When we'd all emerged onto the street afterwards, I'd ignored him, standing there on the pavement in his Dunn & Co. suit, grinning all over his face. He was surely just as proud of me as my mum was. Yet I was covered in a young girl's total embarrassment at his behaviour. I didn't want to be anywhere near him.

'I'm not going home with him!' I'd screamed at Molly. 'Let him get a cab, like he always does. We can walk up and get the bus!'

So that was what happened. Amazingly, Ginger hadn't argued. He just ambled to the top of the high street, deployed his usual loud taxi whistle and flagged a cab down. By the time Molly and I had waited for the bus and got back to the flat, he was in bed. There was no discussion the next day. He was like that a lot of the time. He didn't see anything wrong with it.

But sneaky Pamela Edwards had sussed it: Jacky Hyams's dad was a loud-mouthed drunkard. Something to giggle about with all the others after school.

I was having none of it. I could hide my embarrassment with a bare-faced lie.

'No, my dad wasn't there,' I told Swinging Pony Tail, whom I would eventually grow to detest because she was both good-looking and fantastically athletic, a netball queen beloved by the distinctly mannish looking sports teachers. 'He can't come to those things because he has to work late.'

Of course, Swinging Pony Tail merely tittered and slunk off, damage done.

This wasn't the first time I'd been covered in shame at my dad's drinking. I'd started to be aware of how he was, socially, when I was younger. I'd seen him make a complete fool of himself in front of everyone at a big family wedding. Yet my mum didn't seem to think it mattered at the time.

Well it did matter to me. A lot.

By the time I'd reached Skinners', I was very grateful for the fact that we saw so little of my dad.

He didn't get much time off, other than Sundays, most of which were spent in bed. Back then, Christmas holidays were very short: people just got Christmas Day and Boxing Day off as public holidays, then went back to work (New Year's Day wasn't even a bank holiday until 1974) – and there were big race meetings on Boxing Day. So he'd be off in a taxi early Boxing Day morning.

As for holidays, Molly and I would go to the seaside on the Kent Coast, for a week or ten days every summer – but he'd usually only join us for three days or so, because he had to get back to the business. On those three days, oddly enough, he'd remain relatively sober, a mini drying-out, I guess. It was the after work sessions, six days a week, that the heavy-duty boozing took place.

It's fair to say that I was permanently traumatised by my dad's drinking, although in younger years I hadn't really understood what was going on. It just affected me more and more as I got older.

Some people can drink heavily but they don't seem to change in any way, behaviour wise. Yet Ginger's drinking habit meant that initially he became boisterous and noisy – hence the singing – but then, if challenged or upset about something, he'd get downright angry. Shockingly abusive. The language of the streets.

He'd arrived back from the war in 1946, a skinny bag of bones, his health badly damaged by malaria. A decade on, he was portly and distinctly overweight, and the bouts of malaria ceased to plague him over time. But gradually, the boisterous drunk started to disappear and the angry, bellicose drunk came out – reserving the worst of his routine for when he arrived home.

If I could have avoided him completely, life would have been simpler. But we were in pretty cramped surrounds. If my parents had a conversation in their bedroom, I could often hear it. The bathroom was right next to my bedroom, so that didn't make for very pleasant acoustic, particularly as Ginger was often retching his guts up after an especially heavy night.

I was about ten years old when I began openly to react to all this, run out of my bedroom, start shouting at him, angry exchanges which took us nowhere. But by the time I'd got to Skinners', my loathing for his drinking was nudging open warfare. And, of course, with his neurotic possessiveness around me and my mum, it could only get worse.

Anyhow, being rumbled by Swinging Pony Tail made no difference to my new life at Skinners'. None of the other girls mentioned it to me: gossip is for behind people's backs, isn't it? No one then would dream of openly revealing any upset or dramas of any description taking place in their home, even to friends, so many topics were hushed up and spoken of in whispers.

Many years on I would discover that I was far from the only girl in my year with a troubling domestic environment. A boozy or abusive dad was bad, sure, but on the scale of others' misfortunes, I got off lightly: one girl's family lost everything, including their home, because of her father's gambling addiction; one girl lost a parent to TB (tuberculosis, an illness which remained a scourge in Britain until universal vaccination became available in 1953); another had a parent who committed suicide; one had parents who were divorcing, deemed quite shocking then.

But of course at that age you don't possess the wisdom of years to understand that others too might secretly be nursing embarrassment, emotional pain or worse. All I knew was that my dad's boozy behaviour made us 'different'. What kid wants that?

However, Skinners' itself offered many distractions outside the classroom. Located right in the heart of Stamford Hill, as far as young girls were concerned it had a lot going for it.

There was a huge cinema, the Regent (later called the Gaumont), a salt-beef bar on the other side of the road called the E & A, an amusement arcade (dubbed 'the shtip', a Yiddish word for taking money) and, a couple of years after I started there, a record shop, R & B Records, run by a couple who'd started out running a small stall in Petticoat Lane selling 78rpm vinyl records. They'd spotted the future: the increasing numbers of young kids who were piling in to buy the new rock 'n' roll records.

Molly, once I start at Skinners', is so chuffed about it all, she can't help but regale her best friend, Evelyn, with my 'success' over the phone. This, of course, is not really sensible, since

Evelyn, sharp-tongued and canny, is always quick to jump on any hint of anything negative in Molly's world – and there wouldn't be much good news about my progress over the next few years. But she still issued a rare invitation for us to visit her house in the suburbs one Saturday that autumn. It turned out her son Donald had also passed the eleven-plus and just started grammar school. Evelyn continuously pushed her son towards study, and was determined that he would be successful. (Evelyn won: Don eventually became a doctor).

So off we go on the 38 from Dalston Junction to the Angel tube station, where we stand on the narrow, scary, open tube platform in between the two tracks going in opposite directions (which always terrified me) waiting for the Northern Line train for our journey to almost the end of the line.

Evelyn doesn't have a car, so we have a twenty-minute walk to her house. We know the route – we've done it a couple of times before – but it all feels so alien, the long, long suburban roads with nothing but neat three-bedroom semi-detached houses built in the Thirties, surrounded by open fields and greenery. It's very quiet too after the hubbub of Dalston and the Kingsland Road. There are a few Morris Minors and Austin 7s parked outside the houses. But there's no one around.

Evelyn's semi is welcoming and well decorated, with a very plush dark-blue fitted carpet in the hall and living room, shiny black and white lino in the big kitchen at the back. Evelyn's brothers work in the furniture business, so she doesn't want for anything in that line: there are even framed prints of old buildings carefully hung on the walls, which are perfectly decorated with pale pink wallpaper. It's spotless too: Evelyn, quite gypsyish in looks with curly dark hair, big black eyes, neat pearl earrings and a beautifully cut slim-line flowered print dress, is super house-proud and her kitchen boasts all the latest gadgets, including a big fridge and brand-new washing machine.

'Isn't it great having the fridge, Mo?' she chortles, opening it and removing the covered bowls of salad and tinned salmon which are to be our lunch.

''Spose so,' Molly says, clearly not wanting to discuss anything to do with Evelyn's kitchen, which is so much nicer than ours. As if on cue, the late-autumn sun shines into the kitchen from the large neatly mowed back garden. Everything here seems new, bright and shiny, not old and knackered like Dalston. Even the taps over the kitchen sink are gleaming.

I'm not saying my mum was a slob. She was reasonably tidy and we had Annie, our weekly cleaner, though she was pretty rubbish as well as adept at breaking things: the taps in our kitchen and bathroom always looked grungy, despite her ministrations. Yet the contrast between the poky little flat and Evelyn's immaculate and beautifully furnished semi seems to me quite stark. Even an eleven-year-old can see that. (In 1938, when such semis were first built, they went on sale for the princely sum of £835, with a mortgage repayment of just £4 a month.)

Lunch is eaten in the front room: tinned salmon, tinned Heinz potato salad; lettuce, cucumber and radishes, neatly cut up; Heinz salad cream in a little white dish with a cute serving spoon (not plonked on the table in the bottle, as we did). Bread is a cut-up challa loaf (a Jewish plaited bread, somewhat sweet but tasty).

'So, Mo, how's Ginger's parents?' Evelyn quizzes.

She knows all about us, the two women have shared all the details of their lives since childhood, and she knew it had been The Old Man who had found us our flat just after the war and paid out the 'key money' for us to get us in, before my dad came back from India – at a time when finding a half-decent place to rent in bombed-out London was virtually impossible.

She also knew that Ginger's parents had helped Molly with cash hand-outs and big carrier bags of food from the Lane, when she was struggling post-war on a soldier's wife's pay before his return.

'Oh they're okay, but they're both in their seventies now, so things are getting harder. Miriam's got cataracts but she doesn't want to do anything about them,' sighs Molly.

'Shame they're stuck in those dreadful buildings,' says Evelyn, obviously noticing my grimace at the mere mention of the Lane.

My facial expressions, even then, get me into serious trouble all the time. I don't know I'm doing it. Yet somehow I always give my innermost feelings away.

'Oh, they're not!' I pipe up.

'They want to knock the buildings down and they've been told the council will offer them a nice new place,' I tell Evelyn, repeating what I've absorbed from our last visit.

'Yes, it's called The Barbican, or something,' says Molly. 'But The Old Man says he won't ever move. He says it was good enough for them in the war, so it's good enough now.'

'Poor you, Mo, having to live in the East End all the time,' clucks her friend.

'Any chance of Ginger getting you something nicer now Jacky's at grammar school?' quizzes bitchy Evelyn, knowing full well what the answer will be.

'Oh, Ginge is just like his dad,' sighs Molly. 'If he's working with The Old Man, he won't dream of moving anywhere.'

This was true. Jack and Miriam's hearts belonged to Petticoat Lane and 'the buildings', a state of affairs my dad accepted, but a way of life that bewildered his siblings, who now visited their parents under sufferance.

Yet by the early Fifties there were indeed discussions about demolishing 'the dwellings', redeveloping the area and moving the inhabitants to brand-new housing estates that were being planned in the City. One of these was the Barbican Estate, on the northern edge of what was the old Roman wall surrounding London.

During the Second World War the whole area had been virtually demolished, so it was agreed that the huge forty-acre site was a perfect for creating a huge residential area – and bringing locals back to live in the City of London area.

Today, the Barbican Estate is, in essence, a small walled town with more than 2,000 apartments, also housing the Barbican Centre, the Guildhall School of Music and, interestingly enough, The City of London School for Girls. The Barbican is one of the Square Mile's most historic – and expensive – addresses. Heavily criticised when it was eventually built in the Seventies, the far sightedness of those Fifties planners has to be admired.

Lunch over, now Evelyn wants to show Molly some new clothes in her bedroom.

'DONALD!' she barks loud enough to make anyone jump.

It's an order. Sure enough, Donald emerges from upstairs in shorts and long-sleeved check shirt, tight curly hair just like his mum, and a big grin for us. As usual. He's a very smiley kid.

'DID YOU DRINK YOUR MILK?' Evelyn demands, Gestapo style.

'It's all right Mum, I've had it,' he says, smiling at me and Molly as if to say, 'What is my mum like?'

'SHOW JACKY WHAT PHIL GOT YOU!' orders the sergeant-major (Phil was one of Evelyn's brothers).

'Okay, c'mon Jacky,' he says. He leads, I follow him up the curved stairs to his bedroom facing the garden. Molly and Evelyn are behind us, heading for a peek at her newest outfit – and a chance to gossip without little ears picking up every word.

On the landing shelf you can't miss the big gilt-framed photos of Evelyn, looking super glam in a flowered satin off-the-shoulder evening dress – like the one Molly had when I was little – and Donald as a beaming toddler. No sign of Donald's dad. I'm longing to ask questions. Where is he? Is Evelyn really a tart? But I know enough not to venture forth with such delicate queries.

Donald is the only boy my age I've ever had anything much to do with, though we've only been here a couple of times before. There's my cousin, Anthony, but we were kids when we saw each other – now he's moved to another part of London, so we rarely see him up at Jack and Miriam's.

Donald's room is as neat and tidy as the rest of the house. No train sets, toys or messy boy clutter. Just big pictures of aeroplanes attached to the wall and a couple of magazines on the bed, *Eagle* (a comic, the boy equivalent of *Girl* magazine) and a magazine with more pictures of planes.

There's a little desk with a tiny table lamp and chair in the corner. Piles of paper on the desk. A small electric two-bar heater underneath the desk.

'Is that homework, Don?' I wonder, impressed with his setup. It's all so different to my room, where there's no room for anything much. I do everything – reading, writing – sitting on my bed. We've only just had a new gas fire installed in the living room now that we can't have coal fires any more (the Clean Air Act had just been passed), but I wonder if I should start nagging Molly about my own little electric heater before it gets really cold.

'Mum says I've got to keep working as hard as I can,' says Donald. This doesn't seem to trouble him. Then, still smiling, he opens a drawer and removes an envelope. 'Look, this is what my uncle Phil got me last week for passing the exam.'

It's a piece of paper. On the top are the words Premium Bond. I look at it but don't bother to read the words, until I spot one figure – £50.

'He's given you £50!'

'What you gonna buy?' Wow. Donald has a great life!

'No. You can't spend it, Jacky. You have to save it. It's called a lottery. You keep it and you might win a big prize, like £1,000.'

When Premium Bonds were introduced in the autumn of 1956, these government savings bonds were a revolutionary new concept. The idea was to control inflation and encourage saving.

You could buy a bond for just £1 (the maximum was £500). The top prize was £1,000 – for just four winners a year.

At the time, the average person's only chance of winning a large sum of money was either the football pools or placing a bet with bookies like Jack and Ginger. But the emphasis, as Donald readily understood, was to create savings.

I'm a bit bewildered by all this. Save it? Suppose you didn't win? The whole thing doesn't compute in the 'have it now' programming I'm exposed to all the time.

'We don't need things like that,' I tell Donald. 'My dad's got plenty of money.'

On the long tube ride home, I bombard Molly with questions. Just before we left, Evelyn had opened a kitchen cupboard to retrieve something and I'd spotted shelf after shelf crammed with all manner of tinned foods: baked beans, fruit of all kinds, canned tomatoes, tinned Spam, tinned pilchards, tinned salmon, all kinds of Campbell's soups. If you could put it in a tin, it was in that cupboard.

I had never ever seen so many tins of food in one place. Our cupboard at home never contained more than a few tins of what we'd have for dessert: the odd tin of fruit salad (priced at 1/8) or South African peaches (price: 1/9). I'd never seen cupboards full of tins at Jack and Miriam's. It was distinctly odd.

Why did she need all those tins? She had a big fridge. Didn't she go shopping like my mum?

'She's been saving them, Jac. She says her brother got her lots of black-market stuff when we had the rationing. S'pose she's just kept them – just in case.

'She's got some lovely new things, though. Really expensive dresses and skirts from Jaeger and a lovely Gor-Ray pleated skirt. And some beautiful long leather gloves from D. H. Evans.'

My mother doesn't tell me what else she discovered on that day, figuring it's not appropriate for an eleven-year-old's ears.

But when I'm in my twenties and have left home, she puts me in the picture. That day, Evelyn confided in my mum ~~about her~~ about her relationship with a well-to-do, very generous boyfriend, a much older businessman who lived in the countryside.

With his wife and three kids.

Did that make her a tart? Or a pragmatist? As for the tins, my guess now is it was mostly a hoarder's instinct. Wartime had created all manner of insecurities and fears. Evelyn was surely determined that neither she nor her son would ever want for anything again...

CHAPTER 5

MESMERISED

Bra-less, un-kissed and troubled by my lack of sophistication compared to some of my new classmates, there is one outstanding positive in those first months at Skinners': the arrival of Elvis.

I hear him for the first time via Sandra Holland, my Princess May friend. No real friends yet at Skinners', I go round to see Sandra on Saturday afternoons.

The Hollands live very modestly, renting a shabby terraced house in Prince George Road. Sandra's dad Wilf likes classical music, so their front room boasts an old style radiogram – a combined valve radio and a record player encased in shiny wood, complete with plastic trim.

There's also a black piano, from the Forties, beloved of Sandra's mum, Cath, but for some reason, Sandra's not allowed to touch it.

Pianos, of course, were still found in many homes then: radio, TV and the gramophone had already superseded them rapidly, yet at the beginning of the twentieth century, almost every home that could afford it boasted a piano.

The piano was home – or public house – entertainment of the first order. Piano playing for young ladies in particular had once been considered an accomplishment. In the Fifties, piano-playing recording artists like cheerful Trinidadian Winifred Atwell were hugely popular: she sold over 20 million records through the decade, and was the first black person to have a No. 1 hit ¢ in 1954 with a medley of ragtime songs called 'Let's Have Another Party'.

Cath, busy working part time in a local school canteen, rarely plays these days. Nor does her husband, who, funnily enough, is just like Mr Bessie and treasures his motorbike, spending weekends lovingly tending his precious Triumph Thunderbird. (It was a black Thunderbird that Marlon Brando rode to fame in the movie *The Wild One* in 1953, though the movie was banned by the British censor and remained unreleased until 1968.)

At Skinners' I've taken in everything I've heard about Elvis and his debut sound, 'Heartbreak Hotel', which came out that summer. As Sandra's been telling it, the kids at her comprehensive, Woodberry Down, are getting hold of those very first prized 78rpm Elvis singles, playing them over and over again. Sandra has also managed to acquire one with her carefully saved pocket money.

'We'd better keep it down or my mum'll tell us to turn it

off,' Sandra warns me, removing the prized vinyl disc from its cardboard sleeve and carefully placing it on the turntable.

Click. 'YOU AIN'T NOTHING LIKE A HOUND DOG, CRYIN' ALL THE TIME'! Even listening to him on an ancient player at the lowest possible sound, you'd have to be blind, deaf and dumb not to be propelled, immediately, into the excitement, the raucous urgency of his voice.

I love it. Although my musical tastes, at that point, are unsophisticated, to put it mildly. With no radiogram at home, I've only the radio to hear the same stuff that everyone else hears, the adult music like Doris Day ('Que sera sera') or Johnny Ray, ('Just Walkin' in the Rain').

Elvis wasn't played by the Beeb in those initial days of his fame. But if you tuned in to Radio Luxembourg, the only commercial radio station with adverts and, of course, the Beeb's arch rival – neither ever mentioned the other's existence at the time – you could catch Saturday night's rock 'n' roll fest and Alan Freed, the American disc jockey who featured so heavily in the rock 'n' roll explosion of the mid-1950s. Until Skinners', I'd never heard of Luxembourg, either. But very soon I'd be fiddling with the dial on our radio to catch the magic 208-metres medium wave.

As for TV, it took quite a while before live clips of Elvis in action reached our living rooms. Commercial television arrived in 1955, but pop-music programmes aimed at young people didn't get going until later. So while kids were already enthralled by the exciting new rock 'n' roll music, the jivers and the early American teen movies, at that moment in time, popular music itself was, by comparison, aimed squarely at the adult world.

And boy, was it bland. So the minute you heard this boy with the amazing voice, you knew he was out there, in a class all of his own. No one had ever heard anything quite like Elvis before.

'Got any others?' I ask, offering Sandra one of the last of the Fry's Caramets left in the packet I've almost munched my way through. (Caramets were yummy caramels coated with milk chocolate, a huge favourite then, price sixpence for fourteen: usually I'd scoff the lot in one go, my childhood sugar habit now free to be indulged at whim, with sweets and sugar rationing way behind us by three years.)

Sandra's not a sugar junkie like me. 'No thanks. That's it. There's an LP everyone at school's going on about but I can't afford it.'

I can. I want to buy it but what can I play it on? As I leave, I say I'll see if I can get the album, bring it round. Yet I don't do that. Because I then become far too distracted by the discovery of what Elvis really looks like.

James Dean, of course, had briefly been the hottest young Hollywood pin-up for teenagers – but he died in 1955, aged twenty-four, in a car crash. Sal Mineo, the very pretty young teenager who had starred with Dean in *Rebel Without a Cause*, was starting to draw a huge amount of teen attention and I fancied his baby-faced 'look'. But that was it.

Big Fifties Hollywood names like Paul Newman, Burt Lancaster and John Wayne were slavishly worshipped by millions, yet adult male stars were, mostly, far too groomed and manufactured by the big studios to suit the tastes of the new, young audience in search of someone gorgeously youthful and rebellious to relate to.

Who did we have in Britain? Movie actors like Kenneth More or Richard Todd might have been admired by cinema-going grown-ups. Yet you couldn't say these guys oozed anything remotely like the devastating combo of sex, charisma and That Voice that Elvis offered. He was 101 per cent original AND exotic.

That December, just before my twelfth birthday, I devour all the reading material I can lay my hands on about him, mainly newspaper stories. There are tantalisingly few photos of him in action, but enough to see that at twenty-one, with longish hair and sideburns (a touch of the Teddy boy, but so what?), he's gorgeous, handsome beyond belief. By then, kids in the US aren't just buying the music in their millions, they're already being tempted by a whole range of Elvis-themed merchandise that will not, alas, find its way to Blighty. By 1956, they're buying Elvis-themed record players, necklaces, jewellery, headscarves and bubblegum cards. Even lipsticks like Hound Dog Orange or Heartbreak Pink – 'keep me always on your lips'.

I'm keen to buy lipstick by then. But there's a price issue. There are grown-up pink lipsticks like Yardley's Calypso Pink, but such cosmetics are a bit too pricey for a braless twelve-year-old. A Yardley lipstick costs 7/10. A Max Factor Color-Fast lipstick (with lanolin) in a golden swivel case comes in a bit cheaper at 5/-. But if you wanted the movie-star look, a Max Factor Hi Fi lipstick 'in a gleaming celebrity case', you'd be up for 7/6, way beyond my usual pocket money range.

Seek and ye shall find: I manage to find a more affordable sixpenny half-size pink lipstick from Dalston Woollies. But when I try it out at home, gingerly applying it like I've seen Molly do so many times, examining it all in the mirror of the tiny bathroom cabinet, I don't like the result. It feels rubbery and looks – well, a bit daft.

On my way to school the next day, I chuck it down the metal opening on the landing that leads to the dreadful rubbish chute: smelly and always clogged up, the chute, as I grew up, was a constant reminder that ours was a distinctly ugly environment, let alone dirty. Flies danced merrily around the chute in summer. The local rubbish collectors from the council never turned up regularly to empty the stinky chute from its ground-floor entrance at the front of the building. So the four flights of stone stairs to our flat were usually dirty and rubbish strewn. On the odd occasion, mysterious turds would arrive on the stairs from heaven knows where. There were no pets kept in the dozen flats in the building, as far as we knew. Who was crapping on our stairs?

Molly was inclined to blame Maisie, the ground-floor tyro who hated everyone in the block, reserving extra loathing for the Hyams trio. Molly had suspicions it was Maisie's young son, Alf, the ruffian, making this ugly gesture of – what? – defiance against a tough, uncaring world that seemed to have turned its back on them. We'd never know for sure. Removal of the turds would usually come from Molly or one of our more environmentally conscious neighbours. But their intermittent appearance reminded us that in Hackney, at least, some people didn't care to observe any of the niceties. They just crapped where they stood.

Yet all this, of course, is rendered irrelevant by the discovery of Elvis. We haven't seen him yet – he never does perform here – but the papers call him The Pelvis because the story is, when he sings on stage, he swivels his hips. His body vibrates as he sings, one paper gloats. He shimmers from the shoulders down to his toes, says another. He's obscene because his jerky 'Pelvis' movements are sexy, leading young people astray, another paper proclaims. And he's become so famous, so fast, he's already a movie star.

'There's an Elvis film, it's called *Love Me Tender*!' I exhort to Sandra on one of our Saturday afternoon get-togethers.

So off we go, up to Stamford Hill on the bus the following Saturday to the big Regent cinema, where it's playing. The cinema is packed that afternoon with kids our age. Of course we don't know what to expect – but what we get is somewhat unexpected, a young, sensitive-looking Elvis, looking slightly uncomfortable in his first-ever acting role. It's a Western (bad news for me) and the plot is about the American Civil War, of which we know little, but the minute Elvis appears on screen, the place is in uproar. Lots of screaming and yelling, though Sandra and I sit there, mute, transfixed, not willing to react to what's up on the screen.

He's SO much more in the flesh than what we've read about or heard on the records. I'm mesmerised by his beauty, his cheekbones, that unforgettable smile – and the tender simplicity of the words and the feeling he seems to put into every song. I don't really follow the movie – the stars Richard Egan and Debra Paget are unknown to me, too, though they were big names of their time – but when we come out, I'm stunned when, as we climb down the stairs outside, Sandra says, 'Well, I don't think he's as wonderful as they make out.'

'How can you SAY that!' I blurt out, 'he's... he's... SO LOVELY!'

Sandra just shrugs. She's not an argumentative sort of girl. Nor is she one to express much emotion. We board the bus home more or less in silence.

We have reached a parting of the ways, Sandra and I. Thus endeth our friendship. Neither of us bothers to seek the other out after that.

Back at school, after Christmas, I investigate further. There's a girl in my year, Larraine, whom I met briefly before we started, on the day when we all came to have a look round the school with our mums. She's very chatty, short, with thick dark hair, and gradually we begin to get quite friendly.

She lives in Hackney, near Mare Street, so she gets a different bus home to me. The bus to and from school is, of course, the fastest route to first-year friendships, but so far, I haven't palled up with anyone on the 649 to Shacklewell Lane. There's a gang of girls on my bus, about five of them, who seem very lively. But I'm not sure they'll let me into their little clique. They don't seem very interested in Elvis, either.

Apart from all this, it's taken me a while to find my way around at Skinners'. It seems, to me at least, only used to negotiating such a small space at home, a very confusing building. Lots of different rooms, the huge assembly area, big sports grounds at the back. At first, I just follow everyone else in my year around the place. But now I've worked out the important places where the other girls in my year congregate to gossip during breaks. There's a little gathering spot by a large sundial in the grounds that I now head for after lunchtimes.

I have realised, very quickly, that I cannot stand the school meals, watery over-boiled vegetables, tough, gristly meat, starchy globs of mash dumped on the plate by an impassive catering person with a fag glued to her lips – to this day, I swear there was ash in the food sometimes – all usually left on my plate uneaten, though I note, with amazement, that most girls around me polish off everything on the plate.

Larraine, however, doesn't do this. 'D'you like the dinners, then?' I ask her one day out by the sundial.

It turns out the food isn't quite her thing because her mum's a really good cook and, anyway, Larraine can already cook herself.

This, of course, impresses me greatly. All I can do is stick fish fingers under the tiny cooker grill in our little kitchen. Larraine has a younger sister and a little brother, and her dad, like mine, is self-employed: Monty is just finishing The Knowledge so he can drive a black cab around London.

They live in a council flat and yes, she loves Elvis, has also seen *Love Me Tender* and reacted to him in much the same way I did. Her dad's keen on all kinds of music, loves to put records on when guests come round. So their flat boasts two record players, a big radiogram and a small, recently purchased green-leatherette Dansette record player.

She's already got 'Heartbreak Hotel' and 'All Shook Up'. And the first album. Her aunt gave her some great photos of Elvis cut from an American magazine. She tells me about the magazines you can buy with pictures of him. *Photoplay* and *Picturegoer* magazines (price: 4½d or fourpence ha'penny) soon become our weekly bibles.

Like me, Larraine ties her long hair back at school in a sort of pony-tail style. Mine is already way past shoulder length and is very curly, unruly, a sort of dirty brown in colour. But neither of us – because our hair is so thick and curly – can manage to get it up into that cute, bouncy, swinging look that Pamela Edwards has, the envy of us all: most first years have long, shoulder-length hair to tie up.

'The teachers really seem to like her, don't they? Definitely one of the favourites,' I say.

Larraine agrees: 'The other day, I untied my hair and was just shaking it out before tying it up again, our class teacher, Miss Eckersall looked at me and said, "Who do you think you are, Larraine Gold, Elizabeth Taylor?"'

Much laughter. Even before her scandal-strewn years with Richard Burton, Taylor was one of the best known of all Hollywood glamour babes. To us, it's a back-handed compliment, even though Miss Eckersall is already creating after-class giggles with her odd habit of frequently pulling up her bra strap.

The teachers, of course, are permanent targets for much of our humour. Surnames alone seemed designed for ridicule. I'd had a Mrs Dunnit and a Mr Bullimore at primary. Years later, a Hackney friend recalled a Mr Sparrow (nickname Dickybird, of course) and a Mr Catala (nickname Pussy) at his secondary modern. At Skinners', there was much tittering and snickering around Miss Diaper. Even our games teachers seemed very aptly named, the Misses Rapp and Defty. Both were much older, forties and beyond, and seemed to rank high in the staff pecking order. Sport, as I've said, was taken very seriously indeed.

My contribution to all this physical activity would remain zero, alas. A combination of guile (making up a series of excuses, including forged notes from my parents giving various fantastic reasons why I couldn't participate) and my earliest saddo attempts in the gym – trying half-heartedly and failing miserably to leap over the gym vaulting horse in those first weeks – make it clear to the teachers that it is a complete waste of time and energy to even attempt to encourage me. In that area, I am a complete duffer.

Larraine likes netball. She too is a bit of a reader. She's also been reading *The Catcher In the Rye* by J. D. Salinger, a rite of passage for teenage readers since it first came out in 1951. Holden Caulfield, a seventeen-year-old ex-prep schoolboy, expresses his thoughts on all sorts of things, including the adult world and sexuality – and in so doing, strikes a universal chord with teens everywhere. Even though the setting is America, unfamiliar to us, the confusion of adolescence is depicted perfectly. Perhaps we didn't understand it all at the time. But we certainly got the teenage confusion bit.

Another book we both read was *Peyton Place*, a sensational, somewhat lurid fiction written by Grace Metalious. It made huge waves when it was first published, with its 'hidden' topics of illegitimacy, incest, abortion and murder in a small New

England town. So scandalous was the book at the time of its launch in the US, people were reported to be reading it in secret.

It sold millions all over the world. Then it spawned a successful movie of the same name, which revived the flagging career of Hollywood movie star Lana Turner who played unmarried mum Constance MacKenzie. In the Sixties, it became a very popular TV soap opera.

Not everyone at school had passed the eleven-plus exam easily. Some of the girls in our year were 'grammar marginals', their marks not quite good enough for instant acceptance to grammar school, so they had to have special interviews at the school before any firm decision was reached.

Like me, Larraine got through the exam with flying colours. Yet she had arrived at Skinners' reluctantly. 'It was my mum, she insisted I come here because she knew a woman whose daughter was a pupil at Skinners' and the girl was very clever.'

'If it's good enough for her daughter, it's good enough for you,' Larraine was told. So her fate was sealed.

She too was uncertain about Skinners', didn't like the teachers much. And neither of us was getting any strong guidance from our parents to study, work hard, understand the benefits of the opportunity we'd been handed.

We were girls, weren't we? What was mapped out for us then was marriage, kids. Career was never mentioned. That was how it worked. Perhaps it hadn't worked that way for our teachers. But they were, essentially, light years away from understanding the mores of a group of early teenage girls on Stamford Hill, N16, circa 1956.

We had a role model in our head teacher, Miss Gray. She was a minister's daughter with a degree from Cambridge University. Modest beginnings, though perhaps not quite like ours, but someone for the girls to look up to, to emulate. Yet her generation was so different. Their role in society, as they saw it, was vocational, to pass on acquired knowledge, a noble calling by anyone's standards.

But a noble calling wouldn't help when it came to this new breed of teenage girls. It was a tricky business, teaching girls right at the point of puberty, already distracted by the 'new' consumerism and the temptations of the emerging adult world, girls that hadn't known war or experienced the solid 'do as I say' deference of their parents and the past.

Our teachers, just like our parents, had never been teenagers because their world hadn't come anywhere near to even acknowledging the difference, the vast gap between child and adult.

'They should have understood us,' one contemporary said recently of our Fifties schooldays. My argument is: how could they? No wonder people were startled by Teddy boys, upset by Elvis's body movements that hinted at sex. They'd never known anything like this. It scared the life out of them. Until then, people were stifled by convention, powerful all-pervasive convention that dictated exactly what they could or couldn't do (it was mostly couldn't). Now everything the older generations had known or understood was shifting, changing.

Of course, we weren't all poised to be teenage rebels. Larraine was lively and inquisitive but she wasn't a true rebel; she adored her family. At home she was the favourite, the star, for sure. But as one of three, there were others at home to consider. I was a spoilt only kid who questioned everything, stamped my foot to get my own way and was already engaged in a mini rebellion: conflict with my dad and our surrounds. Yet we quickly bonded, both of us intensely curious about anything to do with books, looks, boys or grown-up behaviour. Like me, she'd never even been kissed.

'Over the points, over the points, over the points, over the points... ' Television was ready to pay homage to the rock n roll phenomenon. *Six-Five Special* – the show started each week with a film of a steam train speeding along to its theme tune, as sung by Don Lang and his Frantic Five – arrived in February 1957, though the Beeb's initial venture into pop-music programming didn't exactly have 'em jumping up to jive in the aisles.

This was the first time rock or pop music acts were ever seen on British television. Yet it was all a bit too timid, though the timing – 6.05pm on Saturday night – was aimed to attract a teen audience. Hosted by Pete Murray and Jo Douglas, the Beeb were very unsure as to how they should be presenting popular music in those early days.

Initially, the music was skiffle-based – hundreds of skiffle groups had recently sprung up all over the country, mostly inspired by Lonnie Donegan's skiffle hit 'Rock Island Line' – but when the producer, Jack Good, became increasingly frustrated with the BBC's insistence that educational or sporting items be inserted in between the pop music, he decamped to ITV a year later to make the pop music show he really wanted, *Oh Boy!* as it was titled.

This time, they did get it right: an all-pop music show for

teenagers which went out on Saturdays between 6 and 6.30pm. Broadcast live from the Hackney Empire and launching the careers of the brand-new British rock 'n' roll stars like Marty Wilde, Billy Fury, and Cliff Richard – all Elvis wannabes, none of whom had much appeal to dedicated Elvis fans – as well as bringing in US artists like Brenda Lee ('I'm Sorry') and Conway Twitty ('It's only make believe'), *Oh Boy!* was a big hit with teenagers, though it only lasted just under a year.

Marty, Billy and Cliff weren't the only home-grown versions of the Elvis phenomenon : Tommy Steele, a blonde lad from south London, with a guitar and a warmly likeable persona, was discovered, like the other Elvis wannabes, playing in the basement of a Soho coffee bar called the 2i's in Old Compton Street. The 2i's was the launch pad for a whole host of British pop and rock music stars and Steele had been the very first with his big hit of 1957, 'Singin' the Blues'.

None of this lot made any impression on Larraine and I. Or, I suspect, a lot of Elvis fans. Who wanted a British version when the Real Thing was so amazing? Especially when the next big Elvis single, 'All Shook Up', seemed set to take over the whole world when it arrived that summer.

That same summer, briefly and intensely, I developed a huge crush on a real live boy. I met Paul just once, when Molly and I visited his family on a day trip to far away Leicester. Paul was eighteen, tall, charming, six foot, brown haired and hazel eyed. He wasn't an Elvis lookalike by far. Or a Teddy boy. He was tidy and conventional. He worked in an insurance office. Yet our meeting, in the living room of his parents' home, which lasted for less than an hour, sent me into a wild spiral of fantasy and longing for months afterwards.

I didn't mention any of this to anyone – not even Larraine. Hope still burned in my heart on the day his younger sister rang me at home, and told me he'd liked me. But nothing else happened.

So all my energies in that direction continued with my fantasy man, Elvis. Photos of him in all manner of guises – a big favourite was in a velvet shirt with long blouson sleeves, though it had serious competition from another shot of him bare chested – were now filling up my world, pictures from magazines like *Photoplay*, *Picturegoer* and, as time went on, a magazine called *Mirabelle*.

I'd sit on my bed for ages, carefully cutting out the shapes of his image, a little tube of Gloy gum with its red stopper at the ready, and sticking the images into the scrapbooks both Larraine and I maintained, religiously, every time we could get our hands on fresh images.

Soon, my wall was festooned with Elvis pictures. This didn't go down well with Ginger who sneered at Elvis, said he was just another greasy long-haired git who'd got lucky.

'Loada rubbish, just like all those Yank kids,' was my father's conclusion. 'You wanna listen to Sinatra. That's what you call a singer.'

Molly said nothing. She was relieved that at least when I was immersed in Elvis, things were quiet.

There were frequent rows with Ginger. Mostly they focused on my determination to avoid the weekend visits to Jack and

Miriam's flat. I'd often flatly refuse to accompany my mum and mostly, I'd get my way, much to Larraine's amazement. She could never imagine defying her parents' wishes in this way and enjoyed visiting her East End relatives.

Yet I was not the only one to seek to avoid the North Flats and its ugly atmosphere. Because of the all-too-frequent standoffs between my grandparents, dubbed the Cold War by my dad's siblings, now married and starting their own families in the 'burbs, they too would avoid the place like the plague if they could manage it.

At ages seventy and seventy-five, Miriam and her toy boy remained locked in permanent combat. Ginger No. 2's wife, Barb, who had married him in the early 1950s when still a late teenager herself, had endured a brief and disastrous couple of months living in the back half of their flat after she and Nev returned from their honeymoon.

'It was awful,' she'd told Molly one day. 'Miriam wasn't a very clean person and she expected me to do her housework. And you'd always hear them shouting at yelling at each other.'

Barb didn't argue with Miriam, she got stuck in with the cleaning. But she had quickly put her foot down with her new husband. This wasn't what she was used to: she'd grown up in a genteel, harmonious family atmosphere in a big house in Clapton. No one swore and no one ever shouted. So the setup was anathema to her.

'If we stay here, I'll go home to Mum,' she warned hubby. Within weeks, Nev had sensibly found them a flat to rent in north London, while they saved for a deposit on a house.

Even if the flat could be avoided, there remained the annual seaside ritual whereby my grandparents relocated for a week or two to their favourite hotel in Cliftonville, Kent, and my dad and his siblings were expected to pay homage, the men usually turning up for a long weekend or a few days, the women remaining in situ in the same hotel with their offspring for the duration.

Since I was a toddler, this seaside ritual had been recorded in our family album of the late Forties, portraying us on deckchairs, Molly in her ankle-strap white wedges and post-war victory roll hairdo, me in a Fair Isle cardie and frizzy hair, Miriam glaring at the camera (probably because Jack was downing double Scotches in the pub).

Jack would pay for everything for his family, so in one way it was a free holiday. And because we were at the seaside, as I got older, it was only in the evenings, when the delights of the beach and the sand were over, that we were obliged to congregate around them.

Barb, especially, hated this family ritual. 'Everything has to be their way, Molly,' she'd sigh to my mum, though Jack's generosity extended way beyond this to him regularly taking Barb, Nev and other family members out for expensive dinners in posh restaurants like J. Sheekey in St Martin's Lane, in London's West End.

In all truth, like most kids then, I revelled in those seaside trips, simply because the water, the seaweed, the sandcastles, the bucket and spade/beach ball rituals were my only connection with outdoor life, the sunny world of nature and fresh air beyond grungy Dalston.

For several years, Molly and I would be collected from our flat by a hired car, often a Daimler, a luxury car, driven by one of Jack's many helpers from the Lane. A man called Dave would transport us, in considerable comfort, all the way down to the Kent coast. The four- or five-star hotels we stayed in were always pleasant and welcoming, three meals a day plus cream teas – and, in my case, all the ice cream cones I could manage. These were our happiest of times. My dad would join us for weekends and many photos that survive call up joyful memories of those earlier days of sand and sunshine.

We were, of course, a part of the post-war British seaside boom. Seaside holidays in Fifties Britain became popular with millions as prosperity and higher wages crept into our lives. People had been entitled to just one week's paid holiday just before the war. Now, by the middle of the decade, the entitlement went up to a full two weeks' holiday with pay.

As more people acquired cars, families could head off in summer on caravanning trips. Holiday camps like Pontins, Warners and the biggie, Butlin's, with their all-inclusive offerings, were hugely popular with families. They offered so much: baby sitting and monitoring, kids' entertainment, all meals, dancing lessons, roller-skating, you name it, the happy campers got it.

It was all a far cry from the traditional East Ender holiday of the Twenties and Thirties, when families would go hop picking in the Kent countryside late August to end of September, staying in farmers' tin or brick huts, sleeping on straw and digging out pits for cooking fires.

Nineteen fifty had seen the birth of the package holiday

when an enterprising journalist called Vladimir Raitz launched Horizon Holidays, offering packages to France including travel, accommodation and food for an all-in price of £32 10s.

This was a real bargain at a time when a scheduled BEA return flight to Nice cost £70. The planes transporting these early package trippers were unpressurised wartime planes that could only fly at low altitude. But it was the beginning of a phenomenon that would change the country's attitude to 'abroad' for good.

By 1959, the emerging sunshine holiday destination of Benidorm, Spain, boasted 30,000 visitors, most of them Brits. Given Spain's incessant sunshine and cheap booze, the British seaside resorts were unable to compete. Yet, nonetheless, the Hyams family stuck determinedly to Cliftonville. His siblings might have ventured further to Spain or France for holidays in the late Fifties, but Ginger was determinedly 'Brit is best'. 'Did my travelling in the war,' he would boast. The truth was, he was terrified of flying. He never had and he made sure he never did.

Towards the end of July 1957, a man with a big moustache and a posh voice made a public statement that struck a very big chord of optimism: 'Most of our people have never had it so good,' Harold Macmillan, the then Prime Minister told a group of fellow Conservatives, pointing out that earnings were up, exports were up and generally, people's standard of living had risen a great deal since those gloomy days of the early Fifties.

It was one of those political statements that everyone picks up on, even kids like me who paid scant attention to politics or anything to do with it.

At home, my dad read what was considered a staunchly Labour newspaper, the *Daily Mirror*, but he was more concerned with what was in *The Sporting Life*, the bookie bible, plus the trio of London evening papers, *Star*, *News* and *Standard*, than anything else, so his voting instincts weren't particularly strong.

Molly, on the other hand, seemed to have inherited a very different view. One of the few things she ever mentioned to me about her Russian father was that he'd been a one hundred per cent Tory supporter. 'He said, "This country should always have a Tory government",' she told me time and again.

Whatever you thought about politics, that never-had-it-so-good phrase stuck in many minds, including mine. It certainly seemed that way in August when Molly and I found ourselves holidaying, for the first time ever, in Broadstairs, Kent.

That year, Ginger had announced that there would be no Jack and Miriam summertime love-in at the Cliftonville hotel. The story was that Miriam didn't really feel like it, what with her cataracts and aches and pains. So Jack had decided they'd be better off with just day trips to the coast. Phew. Off the hook. We didn't know it but the saga of the enforced family visits to North Flats, the Cold War and Miriam's obsessive jealousy of The Old Man was now about to hit the buffers...

I'm on the Viking Bay beach at Broadstairs, posing on the sand, starlet style, in my ruched, elasticated, halter-necked swimsuit, my hair in a frizzy pony tail. Behind me are the tiny beach huts so beloved of the nation and high above, perched prominently over the beach, is Morelli's ice cream parlour – a much-praised

Broadstairs institution, still there to this day, and very much the superstar of this, our 1957 seaside holiday.

Morelli's has the lot: ice cream in tubs or cones, sixpence for a small one, huge sundaes galore at one 1/6 for the greedy teenager. There's a soda fountain, leatherette booths and a juke box too – 'All Shook Up', Paul Anka's 'Diana' and the Everly Brothers' 'All I Have to Do is Dream' – can be played, again and again: everything I want – ice cream and Elvis – under one roof.

This year, there's no chauffeur-driven car. Like ordinary mortals we've arrived at Broadstairs by train from Victoria Station, a long and frustratingly slow journey, especially when, no cabs in sight, we have to carry our suitcases down from the station for the ten-minute walk to our hotel, the Royal Albion. But we don't really mind. It's a new kind of holiday, no Jack and Miriam to tiptoe around while they dominate events, and, for me, another plus, my Princess May friend Kathy Shilling is booked to stay in Broadstairs, too, with her mum and sister, though they're based at a nearby bed and breakfast.

On the beach, Kathy and I lark around, me making faces for the camera, egged on by a laughing Kathy, while Molly smiles, head cocked to one side, in her sleeveless button-through polka-dot dress. Nearby Kathy's young sister Janet, digs, with relevant six-year-old intensity, in the sand. It's idyllic and innocent, a perfect evocation, if you like, of what people so frequently insist was so good about the Fifties: an uncomplicated, gentle, uncompetitive world where the simplest of pleasures, rather than being taken completely for granted, gave maximum joy.

The funny thing is, even in the twenty-first century you can take a summer's day trip to Broadstairs, wander around the place and still find a sense of that uncomplicated, innocent Fifties world. It's a charm that has never quite left the seaside town. Broadstairs remains passionate about Charles Dickens, of course, because he spent much time there and drew so much inspiration from the place. Molly and Ginger would continue to spend their annual summer holiday there for many years.

But for me, that holiday was, in a way, a swansong. I was still a long way off a complete loss of innocence. But not quite thirteen, it was surely the last perfect seaside holiday of my childhood...

We're virtually at the end of the school holidays when my mum announces we're going off to the West End for lunch that Saturday. We're meeting one of her sisters: 'Uncle Syd rang. Rita has just turned up from Kenya, for a holiday – without her husband'

'Typical. Doesn't write, just turns up, expecting everyone to jump' Molly says.

... 'But I'd better go. You'll have to come with me, Jac. The last time she saw you, you were in your cot.'

I quite like Syd, though I've only met him a few times. He smokes a smelly pipe – like many men did back then – and he's good-looking and interesting, quite different to my dad's relatives, who are mostly Cockney East Enders. He was an artist at one stage but now he's got a gift shop. He's got two daughters, cousin Karen, ten years older than me, and cousin Barbara, closer to my age. Barbara's got long blonde hair in plaits on top of her head. One day, when I was quite small, we visited their house outside London. Her sister was away at boarding school that day but we played in Barbara's tent in the garden, a real novelty for me.

'Syd says we'll all meet up at the Corner House,' Molly tells me.

This sounds good. I'd had a Wimpy at a big Corner House when accompanying Molly on one of her shopping trips to the West End and loved it.

'Will we have Wimpy, Mum?'

'No. We're going to the restaurant in the one on Coventry Street. Syd's organised it all.'

It's a funny sort of family reunion. Rita went off to Africa the year after the war ended. She'd been invited there by the parents of her late husband, Hans, who had died suddenly from a brain tumour. In Kenya, she met and married her third husband, an academic. Now, after more than a decade away, she'd come to holiday in Europe: after London, she was heading for friends in Switzerland.

The big Corner Houses in the West End were swish, opulent places with different types of dining on several floors. On the ground floor, you could buy cakes, sweets and deli, order food to be delivered, anything you wanted.

We troop up to the first floor restaurant, an enormous carpeted area with tables dotted all around. It's not crowded so sure enough, we spot Syd and Rita already seated at our table when we arrive.

Rita is tiny, smaller than my mum, super slim – Molly is shapely but her previously trim good looks are now starting to develop into plumpness, thanks to the good living of Bookieworld. Like my mum, Rita's hair is brown and quite thin. But unlike Molly she hasn't had it permed, she is wearing it short, in a neat bob. She's like a little elf in a cream-coloured two-piece suit.

I get a very brief peck hello: 'My Jacky, you've grown up a bit since I last saw you!' she gushes, probably because she doesn't know what else to say.

In turn, I haven't a clue what to say to her but she's even less enthusiastic about greeting her long lost sister. They don't hug or kiss at all.

'Hello Rita,' Molly says flatly.

'Like the suit – made it yourself, did you?'

'Oh you know me, I make everything myself' Rita twitters. 'Poor old you, you could never sew, could you?'

Syd looks at me. He doesn't roll his eyes or grimace, just smiles. He grew up with the pair of them, watching them get their claws out. Rita had never been able to cope with the fact that Molly and Sarah, her two younger sisters, were really close. In turn, Molly has made no secret of the fact that she's not exactly crazy about Rita. Turns out she's never forgotten how Rita sat there, somewhat tactlessly, voicing her big plans for Africa, before the war ended, at a very sad time when their mum lay upstairs dying.

Then the Nippy, the waitress, arrives at the table in her black dress with white apron and little cap. All waitresses at J Lyons teashops and Corner Houses were known as Nippies, nicknamed thus in the Thirties because they nipped around serving people very quickly and we study menus and choose our food: 'just a little salad' for Rita of course, while we order roast chicken, stuffing, thick gravy plus all the trimmings.

Conversation is slow, perfunctory. Syd asks Rita all the polite questions about her life and sure enough, she happily dominates the table talk with stories of how wonderful life is in Kenya, how everyone in Nairobi loves her, including her husband, a real 'me me me' session. No one dares get a word in.

No questions for Molly or Syd, no questions even for me about school. Our food is served and we eat, mostly in silence. Just Rita and more Rita. It could have been quite interesting, this Kenya life, if she wasn't so full of herself, so boastful.

'Oh that Marks and Spencer's in Oxford Street: it's so BIG now! And they've got children's clothes which fit ME!'

'Why can't you just make them, if you're so wonderful at sewing?' I want to yell at her. But of course I stay silent. Then Molly pulls back her chair, somewhat abruptly, grabs her handbag. She's off to the ladies' room, irritated beyond belief.

With my mum gone, Rita, her salad virtually uneaten, puts her knife and fork down and stares at me. It's quite a penetrating stare. A bit unnerving.

'Hmm. Jacky, you do look a bit like our family, eh? But you've got Ginger's colouring. Tell you what, though, it was touch and go with your mum in the war, before she had you. She used to go out dancing all the time. And there was this American, a GI, really handsome, who was MADLY in love with her! He knew she was expecting you, she told him Ginger was away, but he still wanted her to run off with him!'

I stare at her. What is all this? This is gobsmacking news. Have I heard right?

I start to go a bit pink, it's so embarrassing. It's disturbing to Syd too, because he then steps in, stops her before she can go on, repeat any more of this.

'Rita, that's enough. All that war stuff isn't what we talk about here now. Maybe they do that in Nairobi, but we've all had enough of it. Jacky doesn't want to know about all that, do you Jacky?'

I shake my head. It's a very confusing moment for a twelve-year-old, a girl who is so close to her mum. Molly had often chatted about the girls who went off with the GIs, had a good time with them, when she worked in Jax in the war. There was never a mention of any GI in LOVE with her.

Luckily, Syd revives Rita's interest in her favourite topic – Rita – by quizzing her about her travel plans, who she'll be seeing in Switzerland. On and on it goes, Rita, Rita, Rita. She's a big star, is Rita. Marilyn Monroe, watch out. Rita may be flat-chested and tiny, but boy she packs a punch. If only they'd had Twitter then, she'd have had millions of followers.

Molly returns to the table and I'm worried Superstar Rita will mention the GI all over again. But she doesn't. Molly and I order strawberry ice creams from the hovering Nippy and when they arrive in their cute little silver metal dishes, we slowly, carefully, scoop them up into our mouths, happy for the distraction.

Rita, of course, had waved the Nippy away dismissively cooing: 'Oooh, I NEVER eat sweet things.'

Syd just takes out his pipe and sucks. Reflectively.

By then, the table is silent. The two sisters don't want to talk to each other at all. It's all very frosty. Not as bad as the Cold War of North Flats, mind you, where the unspoken threat of aggression hangs in the air, waiting to explode. This is quite different. It's more a sense that everyone, including Rita, wants to get away from the table as fast as they can. You can choose your friends, but you sure can't choose your family, as Harper Lee wrote.

Outside, Syd takes Rita's arm, ready to escort her in the opposite direction to us. Apparently she wants to go to Marks and Spencer to buy those kids' clothes that fit her so perfectly.

We all hug goodbye briefly and then she's gone. Wending her way back to Nairobi where her worshipping fans await her arrival at the airport.

On the bus back to Dalston, Molly heaves a noisy sigh of relief and opens her big black leather handbag to retrieve a Mac antiseptic throat sweet from a packet (as advertised by blonde singer, Joan Regan, who was, puzzlingly to me, at least, a huge favourite at the time). She pops it in her mouth.

'Well, now you've met Rita. She always was a selfish cow. Didn't even ask you about grammar school, Jac – but then, she hasn't got a clue about children, just as well she didn't have any.'

I'm longing to find out more about the GI. Even over a decade after the war, American men retained a powerful, if superficial, glamour, partly to do with the strong Hollywood influence, partly because during wartime in Britain they'd seemed so exciting to young, impressionable women, what with their flash uniforms, strange accents and money to throw around the place.

' Oversexed, overpaid and over here' was the British troops' description of the GI. (The American rejoinder to this was to describe the British as 'undersexed, underpaid and under General Eisenhower'). There were far too many 'Yanks' around as far as the British men in uniform were concerned. They hated the sight of them. Yet the aura around American men had lingered – Elvis was sexy, good-looking and had oodles of charisma. The very fact that he was American, to us, made him doubly glamorous.

I am far too young to ask my mum about something so personal. For a while, I think about it a lot. Me, on the way, but unborn! Suppose Molly'd run off with him? What would've happened? And what about Ginger? He'd have gone crazy.

I'm an adult and have left home by the time I get round to asking Molly about that comment in the Corner House, the only time I ever met her sister Rita.

'Oh Jac, she's such a LIAR,' Molly told me. 'She makes things up just to be spiteful.

'What a thing to say to you, a twelve-year-old! She used to make things up all the time when we were little. She was always in trouble because of it.'

I accept what my mother tells me.

Even if Molly had flirted with a soldier at a dance – perfectly plausible – even if he had fancied her like mad, tried to talk her into bed, promised her the moon and the stars, that sort of thing went on all the time during the war, didn't it? Though in later life, I often wondered what it would have been like to have been born, like some wartime babies, into a life where your real dad was unknown and a moment's madness with a stranger had turned at least two lives upside down for good.

Years later, Rita made an attempt at parenthood. She and hubby adopted a young boy from a troubled background. But it didn't work out. So what did she do? I've no idea how she managed it, but once the boy reached his teens, he was eligible for some sort of assisted passage to work in Australia. For a while, he went to live with Sarah and her family in Brisbane: it sounded suspiciously like Rita, discovering motherhood was difficult, had dumped the boy on... her sister!

Funnily enough, Molly and Rita did meet up again, after my dad had died. In the Eighties, my mum was invited to Brisbane for a big family reunion with Sarah and Rita at Sarah's house, where Rita was staying for a few weeks' holiday. By then, Rita's home was in Canada.

After a few days, Sarah's husband couldn't stand the exposure to Rita's endless ego trip. And both Molly and Sarah became increasingly upset by Rita's habit of running to each sister, in turn, telling tall tales about the other, trying her best to wreck their reunion – and their closeness. They knew what she was like, but being under the same roof as Rita's mendacity was hellish.

It all came to a head one evening when Rita insisted on getting dressed up to the nines to go out to what was, in reality, a dull, unremarkable eating house in suburban Brisbane: dumpy women in ugly floral Crimplene dresses, tubby hubbies in shorts and long socks. Definitely not a place where people dressed for success.

In the restaurant, everyone stared at Rita when she glided in in her tight silk cocktail dress, simpering on cue at the waiters who were hugely unimpressed with such pretentious nonsense. This was dinky di laid-back 'How ya goin' Oz territory, not the Ritz, Piccadilly. It was just, well... embarrassing.

Once they got home, Sarah's hubby lost it. He didn't exactly kick his sister-in -law out. But the next day, an airport taxi was waiting outside the house at dawn.

And Rita's suitcases were on the pavement...

CHAPTER 6

A CORSET

We coughed and wheezed our way through childhood. Bouts of bronchitis and winter evenings inhaling steam from a bowl of Friar's Balsam with a cloth over the head were regular pastimes. A tub of Vicks VapoRub with its familiar blue label retained a permanent place in the bathroom cabinet, its contents rubbed onto a wheezy chest to ease congestion. Galloway's cough syrup was another permanent fixture alongside the brown jar of Virol (malt extract) kept in the kitchen pantry.

Millions of post-war kids recall those remedies with degrees of love or loathing. Yet what is easily overlooked when looking back at the relative simplicity of everyday life in the Fifties – plus the wonder then of having a brand-new free national health service – was the threat to the nation's health from the hazards that were around us. Let alone the shadow of the H-bomb and the increasingly pervasive threat of total annihilation.

Food itself might have been fresher, less packaged, less oversalted or heavily laced with additives back then. The new household refrigerators ushered in a mini revolution in food storage and freezing. Yet there was nothing especially healthy about the air we breathed in towns and cities and, until the mid-Fifties, when new and effective vaccines were introduced, the threat of serious infectious diseases like tuberculosis and polio, which had already robbed many of their health – and sometimes their lives.

That ongoing fear of annihilation had, of course, started at the end of the Second World War in Hiroshima and Nagasaki, Japan, via the dropping of the atomic or A-bomb, killing around 135,000 people.

Then came the era of the real Cold War: the increasingly febrile tension between the Western and Eastern bloc countries, both of whom ensured they had the technology to create and test their own nuclear bombs.

By 1958, such was public concern around the development of nuclear weapons that the campaign for unilateral nuclear disarmament (CND) was launched in London, followed by a historic Easter march of thousands on Aldermaston, the atomic-weapons establishment near Reading, Berkshire.

My dad, a keen follower of popular fiction, bought home a paperback of that year's powerful novel *On the Beach* by Nevil Shute. The book vividly describes a tragic post-nuclear world as experienced by a few remaining Australian survivors who wait for their end via nuclear fallout. It was made into a movie a year later with Ava Gardner and Gregory Peck.

Reading that book made a bit of an impact on me. I didn't discuss the issue of the H-bomb with anyone, not even Molly. It was too scary. So this threat of The Bomb, more than anything else, hovered over my early teenage years. I'd often have nightmares about a nuclear holocaust, particularly later in 1962 when the Russians installed nuclear missiles in Cuba, just ninety miles from the US coast in Florida, and the world seemed to teeter on the very brink of nuclear war. My dreams focused on what the book had described: families like me, my mum and dad at home. Waiting for the end of the world.

Technically, of course, the threat continues, despite all the agreements that were made afterwards to stop nuclear testing. We got used to the idea that no one would be crazy enough to push the button, though nowadays, mass destruction via technology is a terrifyingly fearsome possibility.

Health-wise, I never linked my annual bouts of bronchitis – and a serious bout of pneumonia as a three-year-old – with the environment we lived in. I was just another kid with a 'weak chest'. There were plenty of us.

Not only was our little flat damp and poorly constructed – Hackney, built on marshland, is one of London's dampest boroughs – but coal dust was everywhere.

Not a good idea in a small space.

Coal in the front room and bedroom grate, stores of coal in the small built-in storage cupboard in our bathroom. No one connected this with our respiratory health. Coal or coke was the only way to heat your home as far as we were concerned and, after all, The Old Man had, in a sense, raised his family of five from the proceeds of coal, so why would we question its use?

It seemed our post-war cities, especially London, were intent on choking themselves to death. Those coal fires warming our homes played a big part in it.

Early in December 1952, an evil blanket of black coal-smoke pollution and dense fog descended on London. It blacked out the city for five days. The Great Smog of London, as it became known, led to the entire city grinding to a halt. London Airport (as Heathrow was known then) shut down. Sports fixtures were cancelled. Offices and schools closed. Police walked in front of the few cars or buses crawling along the streets because drivers couldn't see much beyond the car bonnet.

Large numbers of prize-winning cattle, specially transported in trucks to the Smithfield Agricultural Show at Earl's Court, wound up perishing, suffocated in their pens. This was reported in the newspapers at the time – but the effect of the killer smog on the thousands who died from its effects was not reported until quite some time later.

Back then, like other kids, I was stuck at home for what seemed like an eternity.

On the Sunday afternoon, out of sheer curiosity and boredom, I went to our front door and opened it, only to be confronted by a thick yellow miasma, the like of which I'd never encountered. I'd heard the term 'pea souper' fog but the reality was something else. Slamming the door quickly, I ran into the kitchen where Molly was busying herself at the sink.

'Mum, it's YELLOW!' I told her, in childish incredulity.

'YELLOW FOG!' I repeated.

'Stop it, Jac. We can't go out and that's that. There's no racing tomorrow, so I don't know what your dad'll do.'

Ginger was kipping in the bedroom at that point. He'd boldly ventured out to the Lane on the Saturday morning and somehow managed to get home by bribing a very reluctant taxi driver to crawl down the Kingsland Road later on. He too was frustrated at the cessation of normal routines – even his regular Sunday-morning excursion to the Houndsditch boozer had been abandoned that day – so all he could do was use his sober time to rest up.

What we didn't know, of course, was just how lethal that yellow fog was. It even drifted inside buildings. When it was all over, a girl at school told a teacher that her dad had gone out wearing a smog mask. The mask was made up of layers of muslin and cotton wool, all tied over his ears.

'When Dad took it off, it was all brown inside. It looked like Marmite, miss,' she added.

The fog was a serial killer. Twelve thousand people perished in those awful five days, some of whom who had walked, gasping for breath, towards hospitals, only to collapse and die when their pollution-damaged lungs gave out.

As a direct consequence, the Clean Air Act was introduced in 1956. The legislation meant that smoke-control areas were in force in towns and cities, so that only smokeless fuels could be burned, reducing the amount of smoke pollution coming from household fires.

From that point on, air pollution from coal became a thing of the past and heating in homes switched to gas or electric fires, though central heating in most homes remained a distant dream: by 1960 only 5 per cent of homes in Britain would boast a central heating system.

My parents were already overprotective, thanks to that early bout of pneumonia, but after The Great Smog, this fear of the elements increased. Going out in snowy wintry conditions, even when I reached my late teens, was permanent cause for rows and tussles: the general belief was: 'If it's dodgy outside, STAY INDOORS!'

Yet there was another huge health hazard in all our lives, ignored through a combination of public ignorance and commercial opportunism: the smoking habit.

Everyone smoked. Until the war, women hadn't really taken to it, but by the mid-1940s, the habit had taken firm hold with women too. 'Good for the nerves' was the thinking, while some regarded smoking as liberating, a gesture of female independence.

Brands like Weights, Woodbine, Capstan, Player's Navy Cut, Senior Service, Craven A, Du Maurier, Olivier (in a white packet), Balkan Sobranie (black with a gold tip) or Abdulla (oval-shaped, supposedly 'Turkish' but made in London), Embassy and Guards were enormously popular. As were the slick Dunhill or Ronson lighters to accompany them, for those that could afford it.

Weights and Woodbines were the cheapest. Tobacconists – a key feature in high streets all over the country – would happily sell cigarettes singly. Kids too were encouraged to emulate their elders by handing over their precious pocket money to buy kiddie cigarettes made of icing sugar. With a red tip.

The link with smoking and lung cancer started to emerge in newspaper reports after 1954. Yet the tobacco companies remained undaunted – and the public didn't really catch on to the potential killer aspect of the clouds of ciggy smoke that permeated homes, offices, factories, buses, cinemas, pubs and eateries.

Filter-tip cigarettes, many believed, would offer 'protection' from such hazards as lung cancer, so by the late 1950s, many smokers switched their allegiance to filter brands.

Ginger was an early convert to filtered: the distinctive gold Benson & Hedges pack of ten was usually plonked on the living room mantelpiece. He wasn't anything like a chain smoker at that time, yet no self-respecting drinker positioned themselves at the bar without their props to hand. He occasionally smoked cigars at home too: supplies of colourful boxes of top-quality Cuban cigars were also kept to hand by my dad and The Old Man: the association of cigars with prosperity were a talisman, if you like, of bookie pride.

In 1956, cigarette coupons were introduced by a brand called Kensitas. Ciggie coupons had been used to promote cigarette sales pre-war, but the re-introduction of the coupon scheme whereby smokers could 'earn' coupons with the purchase of each pack (just like the traditional collectible cigarette cards), which they'd collect and then exchange for 'free' gifts once, as portrayed in an enticing catalogue, created a mini revolution in the way of maintaining the popularity of smoking.

Our household blithely ignored such incentives, though many kids vividly recall accompanying their mum on a bus ride to the West End offices of the ciggy coupon company, handing over the bundles of coupons collected (often stored on the top of the wardrobe) and waiting until the big moment arrived and they'd 'earned' a new kettle.

The coupon gifts became increasingly generous over time: furniture, washing machines, TVs, record players, sheets, blankets, even driving lessons. In an era where lung disease from tuberculosis still remained vivid in people's minds, smokers would laugh about it: save up enough ciggie coupons for twenty years, so the joke went, and you'd have enough for a free iron lung!

Other coupon touting brands like Embassy cigarettes were hugely popular. By the end of the Sixties, blue Embassy vouchers could even be exchanged for cash, i.e. 10/- for three hundred Embassy vouchers.

Even though the government had eventually started to warn smokers about the health risks, and H.M. Government health warnings were printed on the ciggie vouchers, the 'advice' does seem, to twenty-first-century eyes, quite risible.

'Remove from mouth between puffs' the printed Embassy health warning advised smokers.

By the early Seventies, the anti-smoking message started getting through. Slowly. It would still take far too long for smoke-free public transport and bans on cigarette advertising to emerge, let alone the all-encompassing no smoking bans we have today.

However, ciggie smoke was not the only enemy. Following the 1948 introduction of the NHS, the dentist's chair became a gateway to a chamber of horrors for many kids in the Fifties.

As a toddler I'd had teeth extracted under a nasty general anaesthetic. It was a ghastly experience. The sinister rubber mask, the scary sound of hissing gas, waking up feeling sick and woozy, left me, like many others, with a permanent determination to avoid dentistry at all costs.

Unrealistic, of course, but trauma stays with you. Today, an experienced dentist well versed in dental history will tell you that older British teeth, especially amongst those over sixty, are generally bad because of poor dental education and inefficient or over-zealous NHS dental treatment in the Fifties.

Moreover, when free NHS dental treatment also became available in 1948 (a flat-rate fee of £1 for dentistry was introduced in 1952), many adults opted to have all their teeth removed whilst still relatively young, i.e. in their thirties and forties. That's why there were many people with false teeth in Britain in the 1960s and beyond.

Our emotional health wasn't too healthy either.

If diseases like cancer, TB or polio surfaced in families, there would usually be whispers, hushed conversations – another example of the way the more distressing or difficult aspects of life were turned into shameful secrets – when what people needed most of all was support, information and communication to help them cope. Or at least understand what was happening. Yet in an era of deference, doctors were up there with the gods: whatever they told you, few would dare to question their wisdom.

By the autumn term of 1957, I'd moved up to my second year at grammar school. This was the really the point when my time at Skinners' started to spiral downhill. Before, I'd been a newbie, 'casing the joint', working out how the school itself operated, who my friends might be, which teachers were the most unpleasant (sadly, most of them, though my relationship with our class teacher, Miss Edgar, remained cordial throughout, probably because English was her subject and she could see, despite my obvious indifference to study, homework, that this was an area where I could take off – if I only took the trouble).

But now I was far too focused on life outside the classroom, eager to move into 'grown-up' behaviour, given that some of my more precocious classmates seemed so far ahead of me.

My first very tentative steps towards socialising with local boys started that autumn, when Larraine and I shyly made our first evening visit to a nearby Jewish youth club, the Stamford Hill Club, situated on 'The Hill' as it was known, not far from our school. Carefully kitted out in neat little fully fashioned cardigans, wide plastic belts cinched at the waist and full skirts with zany patterns, flat pumps and curly pony tails, we gingerly made our way into the main area of the club.

There was entertainment in the form of a table tennis area, plus a sort of bar with soft drinks and, of course, a central area for dancing to records played on a Dansette.

'YEW ARE MY DESTINY' Paul Anka warned us 'THAT'S WHAT YEW AAARE.'

Would our destiny be one of the motley crew of mostly spotty fourteen- or fifteen-year-old boys in hand-knitted woolly jumpers and cheap trousers with turn-ups who stood, nursing their Cokes, nervously watching us on the other side of the tiny dance area?

Not a chance. It was a pretty awful start. We stood, we

watched, we waited. No sign of a curled lip, sexy Elvis lookalike or even a James Dean doppelgänger among the local talent.

No spotty face came over to ask either of us to dance as a few couples, already established as teen sweethearts, took to the floor and either shuffled carefully to the slow ones or jived in neat synchronicity to Larry Williams's 'Bony Moronie', followed by a heavy duty blast of 'Lucille' from crazy Little Richard, the explosive black singer who'd been making big rock 'n' roll waves since the raucous cry of 'Tutti Frutti'.

No one even spoke to us. Unacknowledged and ashamed of our failure, we were in and out within an hour, our tiny teenage egos dashed to bits.

Larraine didn't know it but I still couldn't jive properly, so I had no game plan for what I'd do if it was a fast one and someone did ask me. Nothing at all about our venture seemed in the least bit promising.

'They all seemed to know each other, didn't they?' Larraine remarked wistfully as we walked somewhat glum faced towards our respective bus stops.

'Yeah, d'you wanna go again?' I asked her.

Neither of us dared voice our greatest fear – that no boy would ever want to dance with us, let alone kiss us, two physical opposites, Larraine, short, dark-haired and exotic looking, me taller, quite skinny with pink (though unblemished) skin.

'Dunno,' came the response. 'My dad thinks we're too young to go to the club, anyway.'

Her dad Monty was right. (Ginger, of course, wasn't even appraised of this new development; by instinct, my mum and I knew to keep it under wraps). Our theme tune that first night, Larraine already thirteen, me weeks away from that birthday, is best summed up in the title of Ricky Nelson's hit song, 'Poor Little Fool' (Nelson, seriously cute, and a successful US TV star, was just sixteen when he made that record, dying tragically young aged forty-five in a Texas plane crash).

Dancing – or rather, patiently waiting for a boy to ask you to dance – had been the traditional first stop on the route to courtship and marriage for a long, long time. Our parents' generation had met and courted in the big dance halls found in cities all over the UK, or attended small local hops. The huge London dance halls like the Streatham Locarno, Tottenham Royal, Hammersmith Palais, or the Lyceum in the Strand were incredibly popular before and during wartime. By the early Fifties, they retained their popularity, with millions visiting them each week, second only in the entertainment stakes to the huge cinema audiences at that time. You had to have some idea how to waltz, tango, foxtrot properly back then; you couldn't wing it just shuffling in time to the music. Yet ballroom dancing itself was pretty much a pre-war thing: by the mid-1950s its appeal was increasingly middle-aged.

In so many ways, these big halls of courtship were the dating sites of their day: in 1962, 75 per cent of couples claimed to have met on the dance floor. But they could be somewhat nerve-wracking for those lacking in confidence: the young man, spruced up in a suit, shirt and tie, shoes polished, summoning up the pluck to risk being told 'no' in front of his mates when he'd approached a likely partner; the young girl, equally 'done up' in Saturday-night finery, waiting hopefully for someone nice but also risking total rejection – as we had.

We never visited the big dance halls like the nearby Tottenham Royal. The word at school was, the Royal was quite 'rough'. But although my dancing life started, with trepidation, at the Hill club, graduating later to coffee-bar basements, then more sophisticated West End discotheques, I would never learn to dance properly, ballroom style.

In time, I could manage a gentle jive, nothing too frantic, but it was a bit of a relief when the twist came on the scene at the end of the Fifties: you could wiggle your hips and improvise with the twist. Do your own thing, opposite your partner; you didn't have to follow your dance partner's lead with all your steps. Very liberating.

Nevertheless, within six months of that miserable night of failure, I'd graduated: finally, I was wearing a bra. I'd sprouted enough up top to warrant a Kayser Bondor bra, purchased from Jax in Dalston Junction with my mum's help, and acquired two pairs of seamless nylon stockings, also from Jax, held up by a little white suspender belt. While it was still socks and lace-ups from Pruim in Stoke Newington, or Mary Janes for school, I'd also acquired my first-ever pair of black kitten heels from Dolcis, the very popular high-street shoe chain (along with another big shoe chain called Bata), both chains long vanished from view in the UK, though Dolcis still sell their brand online.

When Larraine and I make another attempt at visiting the Hill club, we both get asked to dance. Slow ones.

I get David, a skinny, cheerful, curly-haired boy who tells me he goes to Grocers. He lives on the Clapton side of the Downs. His mum works on a stall 'down Ridley', his dad in a factory making suits.

Larraine, to her utter astonishment, gets asked by Handsome Malcolm, who every girl in the club fancies like crazy. He really is a looker: thick dark hair, Elvis-style, perfect profile. But heartthrob Malcolm glides off to play table tennis after the Teddy Bears' 'To Know Him is to Love Him'.

'Think he's got a steady girlfriend' Larraine excitedly tells me. She's already in love.

That was all it took sometimes: two slow dances. Well, you did get quite close, after all, though there was no whiff of aftershave in the close-up: brands like Old Spice or Brut didn't start to appear in young men's bathroom cabinets until well into the Sixties. You were more likely to get the pong of sweat mingling with tobacco; these boys didn't use deodorant, I doubt if they even knew it existed. Let's face it, most of them were still only going once a week to the local baths. If that.

I'm definitely not in love. David, teen opportunist, might be a grammar-school boy but he isn't anything like my idea of a catch. I remain totally Elvis fixated: my feelings later best summed up by a besotted Dolores Hart in Elvis's fourth – and best – movie, *King Creole*, when she tells him, 'I like you more than anybody I know. And I don't even know you.'

How could a schoolboy in a very badly knitted jumper compete with all that? Yet David dived straight into the local courtship ritual with a broad, cheeky grin: could he see Jacky home?

'Nah, I'm staying at my friend's,' I tell him.

This is a lie. I did sometimes sleep over at Larraine's home. Her sister Adrienne would obligingly move to the 'Put-you-up' in the lounge so we could share Larraine's room, giggling endlessly and chatting about girlish nonsense into the wee hours until we finally nodded off. But I don't care to encourage Bad Jumper. The night itself is a small triumph for both of us: now we're known at the club.

Being known at the club, of course, was just one of a series of significant steps towards adulthood. Yet there were times when I found myself rejecting certain elements of grown up womanhood. For instance, in acquiring the stockings and suspender belt I'd learned something quite surprising after flicking through newspaper adverts: women then were still being encouraged to wear full-length corsets, boned, fitted undergarments that held you in place – yet seemed designed to restrict your every movement.

Molly had even enquired as to whether I wanted one of these corsets to hold up the new stockings. She'd worn versions of a style of corset or girdle since her youth, of course.

I was horrified at the suggestion. 'Mum, it's too tight,' I told her, without even wishing to try one on. I'd had enough of restriction. As a toddler, there'd been the Dreaded Liberty Bodice to contend with, the sleeveless alternative to a corset for kids – complete with hideous rubber buttons – that was apparently designed to keep your chest warm. That was bad enough. The idea of being grown-up was to be free, wasn't it?

I thirsted only for freedom. Being cooped up in a

claustrophobic flat didn't help, for sure, but that compulsion for freedom was also an instinctive part of my personality. Your parents, whose wishes you have no choice but to fulfil as a child, evolve into jailers once you aim to experience the world away from them.

Emotionally, there's so much going on: the increasing desire to make some sort of an impression on the opposite sex, the need to look the way you think you should look. Plus, of course, the bewildering but driving distraction of what attraction to certain boys really means. We knew it meant this thing called sex – but what did 'making love underneath the apple tree' really MEAN?

I'd experienced physical attraction in a minor way with Paul, but now all I had was the faraway idol. Larraine and I had, by then, screamed our heads off in the Hackney cinema when Elvis's new movies tore the screen apart, first in *Loving You*, then a few months later in the fabulous *Jailhouse Rock*, designed to exploit his incredible talents – and looks – to the max. *King Creole* would come later that autumn of 1958, timed to maintain Elvis's popularity once the US Army decided it was time to cut his hair and curtail his movements.

We didn't quite know why we cried out at every curled-lip or hip movement. He was exciting, we were acknowledging his sexual power, though oddly enough, through everything we heard about him much later, the real Elvis was, back then, not exactly a sexual athlete. He denied, publicly, that his hip movements related to sexuality; they were just part of his relationship with the music. It could have been hype, of course, but it was believable at the time.

It turned out too that by all accounts, he was a conservative lover, despite the stunning array of female talent at his behest. Possessively insecure, a boy whose appearance meant so much to him even before fame came along, he dyed his hair black right from the word go.

By the time he'd dazzled us with *King Creole*, of course, he was in Germany, off the scene, as it were, though there were plenty of photos of him at various stages of his induction into the Army, in particular of the big hair-cutting session which was, to us, terribly cruel. Would we stick with him? From the minute he'd arrived there were dire predictions that he – and rock 'n' roll – were doomed. It was all a flash in the pan, they said. The kids were fickle. They'd be wanting some other kind of music very soon.

No chance. Elvis had provoked something incredibly powerful in the teen psyche. A voice that spoke to teenage longing, even to those of us who couldn't really imagine anything on a truly sexual level. I was still stuck at the 'want to be kissed' stage, knowing so little about what really went on beyond that. But that too was poised to change while Elvis was in the Army. Thanks to Bad Jumper, incredibly enough.

The girls I knew at Skinners' who were far more knowledgeable than me included the little gang who were my travel companions on the trolley bus home.

Sylvie and Barbara were sisters, a couple of years apart, who lived near Hackney Downs with their 'separated' mum (rumour had it she was divorced, which was pretty much 'mention it if you dare'). Sylvie was in my year, a sunny, outgoing, cheerful girl who worked really hard in class but could never hope to emulate Barbara, who was super smart, derided study but always got good marks.

Barbara was a direct opposite to her sister. Sullen and quite mysterious, she fascinated me, mostly because she'd make intermittent but darkly knowledgeable comments about boys, hinting that she knew a hell of a lot more than the rest of us. The rest of their gang, Heather, Linda and Rosalind, were nice Jewish girls, polite to the teachers, unremarkable in class, already intent on snaring a local boy for matrimony: Heather was going steady with an older boy, Mike.

This was not unusual: there were others at school that were unofficially 'engaged'. Mostly, for me, the most interesting of the group was the renegade Barbara: perhaps I identified most with her, though I had not yet reached my peak as a sullen, sarky teen.

I couldn't identify with the others. A plan to snare a boy for life was just not on my agenda: I wanted to be wanted, like all teenagers. But wanted as a potential wife? What for? Why did they so long to be wives? There were plenty of other things to do in the world, weren't there?

Perhaps some of Molly's lack of total dedication to home making or housewifery had already rubbed off on me. Yet many working class girls then, of course, were intent on fulfilling their destiny. We were all expected to pair off quickly, produce children and, later, grandchildren. Career? Well, it was a good idea to work before you married, help save up for a home. But once children arrived, this generation were more or less expected to be where our mothers were – at home, taking care of the family.

I wasn't quite under the same sort of unseen pressure to conform to the Nice Jewish Girl Gets Engaged Quickly stereotype. A combination of my dad's very anglicised family background – people acknowledging their Jewishness without seeing any need to conform rigidly to all Jewish mores – and my mum's somewhat fractured family story, with siblings marrying 'out' and wartime ruptures upending all normal life, meant that being Jewish, living in a Jewish area, attending a school where many of the pupils were Jewish, was an accepted fact of life. But that was it for me.

By then, my own decisions about it all were shaping up: a loner child, I had no wish at all to be part of an ancient group, doing things everyone else in the group did because your long history and traditions bound you together.

This held no appeal whatsoever. Religion aside, being part of a group at Skinners' where discipline, study and at least outward respect for your elders were part of the deal, could never work for me either. Being so used to getting my own way, ignoring all else, knowing my dad used an openly risky bending of the rules to maintain our existence, I was already quite a good candidate for rejecting authority. Why would I conform to school rules and regulations? There wasn't much real discipline at home. I'd already discovered I could use my stays at Larraine's place to come home later than my dad would insist, though in truth we didn't hang around until very late after our forays to the local club.

Skinners', with its solid traditions, had a whole range of strict rules on behaviour outside the school.

The school beret, for instance, had to be worn at all times on the street with the school badge prominently displayed. Sensible girls in my year would merely fold the beret into quarters, pin it on and just ensure the badge was visible. I couldn't be bothered with that. I just shoved it in my pocket at every opportunity.

Eating outside or around the school was also verboten. Stamford Hill had an array of shops opposite the school and in my final year, a Wimpy Bar appeared, though munching burgers in the street was a step too far – even for me. However, the E & A salt beef bar, on the other side of the road, held cheaper takeaway temptations. Yummy pickled cucumbers could be purchased for pocket-money pennies. So by my second year, I'd often manage to persuade Larraine to join me in a cucumber munching session after we'd finished classes. Without our berets.

Punishment for ignoring the Skinners' beret rule was Victorian: if caught, you had to wear the offending beret in school, in assembly and in classes, throughout the day, a sort of 'wear the dunce's cap' treatment of the offender. It wasn't that easy to catch any pupils eating in the street. You were unlikely to encounter any teachers, unless you were really unlucky. Of course, there were always prefects around to dob you in. Nonethess, I successfully avoided the punishment of the all-day beret.

One afternoon, showing off to the other girls, I chucked the hated beret out of the top-deck window of the bus home and watched it fly away into the hinterland of Stokey. Of course, everyone shrieked with laughter.

'Get off, Jacky!' Sylvie urged me.

'Go and find it!'

I shrugged. 'Nah, not worth it. I'll just say it got lost.'

So that was what I told the teacher when I was hauled up, beret-less, later on. Naturally, that didn't work. A letter was promptly sent home, politely asking my parents to purchase a replacement, which Molly did, bravely fronting the snotty Kinch & Lack man in Victoria once again.

'What did your mum say?' asked a somewhat shocked Larraine.

'Oh she just went and ordered it. She wanted to go up West to the shops anyway,' I told her without any sense of guilt.

We should have had the famous Catherine Tate 'Am I Bovvered?' slogan back then. Because that was exactly my response to any school attempt to discipline me, make me toe the line.

I regarded the old-fashioned teachers, the ridiculous rules and most of my grammar-school education with little more than scorn. I paid a bit of attention in English and French classes. We had a good French teacher too – Miss Watson – and her enthusiasm for the language was infectious. But other than that, I was indifferent to study or games, frequently sullen or sarky to the teachers.

I'd do it for laughs, to an extent, and I wasn't troubled by being given detention or bad marks – or even being hauled up in front of the class.

Larraine, whose biggest problem was that she was far too talkative in class when it was wise to shut up, would be troubled by the idea of being singled out for criticism. Not me. I didn't give a toss. If I'd been contrite when hauled up for thumbing a sexy Harold Robbins book and giggling over it at the back of the class (Robbins was a hugely successful US fiction author at the time who wrote about taboo topics like sex and prostitution: Elvis's movie *King Creole* was based on a Robbins' novel called *A Stone For Danny Fisher*), perhaps the teachers might have felt they'd made their point. But contrition – or even pretending remorse to smooth things over – was way beyond me. Why pretend?

At the heart of it all was always the Big Question: Why?

Fine to ask why as a child, I guess, even if the responses are sometimes unsatisfactory. Kids often ask questions all the time. But for an early teen, the Why should I? factor merely edged me towards rebellion.

Being a 'why' kid also made me very nosy at home. I always thirsted for further knowledge.

One day, I realised that the bigger wardrobe in my parents' bedroom, the one housing my dads' suits, coats, and ties, also had a few compartments at the bottom that housed other items. What the hell was in there?

Wardrobe Snoop waited until both parents were safely out of the flat.

Then she raided. Mostly, the raid yielded those thin blue airmail letters with the edges that you had to stick down. People used them during the war and beyond and I found many letters to my mum from my dad in India. I won't say they were love letters but the sentiments expressed were of utter devotion – a word that also cropped up frequently on the photos my dad sent my mum from India – and love for my mum and me, then the child he had yet to meet.

My dad wrote well, he could express himself with the pen in ways you wouldn't expect from someone who'd left school at fourteen, spoke with a strong Cockney accent and even seemed, as he grew older, to delight in all the slang and dropped aitches of his lingo.

To meet him as he was then, a Fifties bookie, a real 'cor blimey' sort of guy in his late forties, a typical East Ender, you wouldn't have cast him in any other role. Yet in those letters, written from far away, the younger Ginger was lucidly and keenly romantic, writing vividly worded descriptions of his exotic surroundings. He'd sent many photos too, so we'd been able to see some of it. Beautiful white buildings. Smiling men in turbans. End-of-war celebrations with garlands around his neck. In Dalston, it all seemed quite glamorous and exciting.

I wish I still had those letters. The photos survived. Yet the letters were destroyed in a big chucking-out session years after Ginger's death.

But were other things in that wardrobe, things I could not identify.

I found a packet of Durex. I didn't understand what this meant and I didn't dare open the little packet. What was this all about? The wording on the packaging didn't help: 'protection' it said. Protection from what? Rubbers, they used to call them and rubbery they were, none of the 'pleasure max' on offer today, though at the time, 60 per cent of married couples used them to prevent pregnancy.

A couple of months later, I gleaned the information I wanted, via one of my bus conversations with the egregious Barbara. I even hopped off two stops early to walk down the road with her and ask her about the packet.

'Yeah, it's what men put on when they do it to stop babies,' was her somewhat succinct response, revealing disturbing news about my mum and dad: who really wanted to know what their parents did in the night? The thought that my mum and dad still 'did it', this mysterious act that was only whispered about but brought babies, was one I shrank back from. Not in horror, exactly. More in fear of what I didn't really know or understand about sex.

I knew enough from the books I'd read that people 'did it'. But I had never ever connected anything I'd read with my mum and dad. I was their child, so of course they'd done it. Once. Why were they still doing it?

But it wasn't just the little packet of condoms tucked away at the back of the wardrobe. There was also a very strange rubber object that really flummoxed me. It was a softish rubber cup shape with a round rim. You could sort of see through the rubber. What on earth was this? What could you do with it?

I was so scared of this peculiar find, I'd hesitated to ask even the worldly Barbara what it was when grilling her about the Durex. I kept my discovery all to myself. In my innocence, I didn't connect it with what the Durex was for. To me, it seemed to be connected with some hideous medically related venture. It would be quite a while later that I would understand it was a cervical cap, a contraceptive device that had been in use by women since the Twenties. Contrary to popular belief, women's contraception didn't start with the Sixties and the pill. It's as old as the hills.

So my wardrobe raid revealed that there were mysterious private goings-on between my parents that nosy teenagers asking too many questions might not necessarily need to know.

By that time too, Hackney's residents were taking advantage of more mundane innovations, even if they couldn't afford to buy them for the home. The first ever self-service coin-operated launderette had opened in Bayswater in 1949. Two and six for nine pounds of dirty washing. By the mid-1950s, launderettes were sprouting up everywhere.

Hackney's first public launderette was launched in Clapton, to great fanfare, in January 1958. Twenty washing machines and six spin dryers. Real liberation for hard-pressed widowed mums working six days a week for a pay packet of around £6 a week.

My mum, when I mentioned the Clapton launderette, didn't seem to show much interest. But then, she and my dad had acquired a far-too-serious Lush & Cook or Achille Serre habit to bother about it. (Like Achille Serre, Lush & Cook was a well-established high street chain, now long gone, offering pricey laundry and dry cleaning services.)

Green Shield Stamps were another innovation that appeared, briefly, in our home. Based on an American idea, this was essentially an early rewards-cum-loyalty scheme. Shoppers were handed a number of little green stamps bearing the Green Shield logo, depending on how much they had spent, by retailers participating in the scheme. As with the cigarette coupons, customers could save the stamps, stick them into a little booklet, and eventually exchange their books of stamps for all manner of goods.

When it was launched, the award was one stamp for each sixpence spent (roughly two and a half pence in today's money). Each book contained 1,280 stamps, so you needed huge numbers of books to acquire a big item.

Green Shield Stamps became hugely popular in the Sixties and Seventies as increasing numbers of retailers, big and small, participated, and initially, Molly did start collecting them – but for some unknown reason, she lost her enthusiasm. (Green Shield Stamps eventually vanished in 1991.)

One day after school, I confided in Larraine about my discovery of the Durex and told her what Barbara had said. To my utter amazement, she said, 'Oh, my mum and dad do it sometimes.'

'How do you know?' I said, quite astonished.

'They sometimes say they're going for an afternoon nap,' my friend told me.

'One day, my dad left a note for us on the bedroom door: "DO NOT DISTURB", but my little brother, Keith, knocked on the door, yelling, "DAD! WHAT DOES DISTURB MEAN?"'

So there it was. Her mum and dad were doing it, too. 'D'you think they use the Durex?'

'Don't know. But I know my mum had something called a miscarriage once, when I was small and we were living in the prefab.'

Like many bombed-out Hackney families, Larraine's were housed post-war in a prefab, a fast solution to the severe housing shortages of the time. Pre-built in a factory, these concrete homes with aluminium, steel or wooden frames were relatively easy to erect. The original plan was to build 300,000 prefab houses. In the end, just over half that number were erected in the years between 1945 and 1951.

Prefabs were built to last a decade. Yet many prefab estates survived way beyond that, even into the twenty-first century. These 'built in a day' two-bedroom family houses spelled luxury for some families – because this was the first time they'd had an indoor toilet.

The country's battered landscape was now changing in many other ways. As more families started to buy cars – car purchase would tip five million by the end of the decade and spending on cars and motorcycles quadrupled – the very first parking meters had been installed in London in 1957. And the bombsite, that all-familiar scar of the war, had already started to take on a new role: as a car park.

The NCP car-park empire started in London in 1948 when two ex-servicemen paid £200 to purchase a bombsite in Red Lion Square, Holborn, and convert it into a car park. At the time, it was seen as a very risky venture since there were so few cars on the road. By 1958, following the acquisition of several more bombsites around the UK, National Car Parks was born: Europe's largest car parking organisation.

But despite all those new Morris Minors and Austin 7s appearing on the roads, London's public transport still played a central part in most people's lives.

Travelling back and forth to school by bus was de rigueur

then, parents didn't drop off or pick up their offspring from school the way they do now. Nor were there specially laid on school buses for kids.

What this all started to mean, of course, was a developing freedom to roam. Ginger might have been possessive, but our parents didn't worry on Saturdays if me and Larraine went off in the daytime to the West End, travelling by tube or bus: provided we were home at the appointed hour, kids travelling around London by public transport was normal, accepted. With my intense inner desire for greater freedom, I didn't realise or acknowledge it, but here was a gateway to escape, if you like. We lived in a place where there were buses going everywhere, in every direction. Journey times were much shorter then, nothing like the traffic on the streets that exists today.

In the autumn of 1958, after Elvis had gone to Germany, we were called to assembly one day for a special announcement. A new girl would be starting at the school.

'She is not from these parts,' our headmistress, Miss Gray, told us.

'You must all treat her with courtesy and consideration.'

This was Skinners' first black pupil, a thirteen-year-old girl called Efe.

Skinners' was forbidding enough to new entrants from Hackney, let alone a young girl from an African country, though we never did learn her real origins or family background.

How strange it must have all seemed to her, the big Victorian building, the mostly stern teachers, the classrooms of ebullient and lively white teenage girls. She was terribly shy, surely intimidated by it all and though quite a few of us approached her outside class, wanting to be friendly, trying to draw her out, she said very little to any of us. It was never going to be easy, yet within a month or so she was gone. No explanation from our head. It just hadn't worked out.

By that time, Britain's black immigrant population had started to grow steadily. From the Fifties and into the Sixties, a mass influx of workers arrived from the Caribbean in London to fill jobs in hospitals, on buses and railways. African students seeking to study here arrived too, followed by doctors from the Indian sub-continent to fill vacancies in the health service.

Yet my time at school was one of huge racial prejudice and harsh attitudes, culminating that summer of 1958 in Notting Hill when mobs of Teddy boys roamed the streets housing black immigrants, jeering and taunting them, attacking their houses, the taunts turning to riots and violence. Bricks were hurled at the police and one man was slashed across the neck: in the end, nine white young men, ringleaders, were given five-year prison sentences.

London, of course, was no stranger to immigration, particularly the East End, traditionally home to large populations from many other countries including the Irish, the French Huguenots, then later huge numbers of Jewish people – just like my fleeing grandparents – on the run from persecution from Russia and Eastern Europe in the late nineteenth century.

The arrival and departure of a lone black girl at our school underlines how few black families there were then in our area, though this would very swiftly change in the next two decades as the city's cultural mix started to develop even further and today encompasses virtually every background, every part of the world you can think of.

Back then, Britain itself was not a comfortable or welcoming place for those whose background marked them as 'different'. 'No coloureds,' said the signs in the windows of inner city boarding houses. 'Jewish household,' said the *Hackney Gazette* classified ads for those seeking a room or flat to rent in the late-1950s. In other words, 'we'll stick to our own, thanks', not entirely surprising given that six million Jewish people had been systematically exterminated in the Holocaust less than two decades before.

It's true of those times that discrimination of race, religion, class, sexuality and gender maintained a very strong grip on the nation during my Skinners' years. Until 1960, a young woman working in the Civil Service, for instance, had to resign if she wished to marry. The divorce laws discriminated heavily against ordinary women until legislation finally changed in 1969 and the 'no fault' divorce became law. Ruth Ellis was the last woman to be hanged in Britain in 1955 – yet it was only in 1965 that capital punishment ended. Gay men could find themselves in prison, until the decriminalisation of homosexual acts in 1967.

Another reason why the rose-tinted view of Britain's post-war era sometimes requires a far more thoughtful examination...

CHAPTER 7

END OF AN ERA

I'm studying the cover of *Photoplay* magazine intently. There's a big picture of Elvis in Army uniform and cap and underneath it says: 'Elvis's last words to you before going overseas: "Please don't forget me when I'm gone."'

As if...

Just as I'm wondering where I've left the little pair of scissors I use to cut such images out for my wall, the door to my room opens and Ginger stands there. Home quite early tonight, still in his street gear of smart suit and neatly pressed shirt and tie, he looks quite sheepish. There's a small black box in his hand.

'This is from The Old Man,' he tells me, placing the little box on the bed. 'He wants you to have it for your birthday.' Then he's gone, knowing all too well I have no desire whatsoever to indulge in any further form of conversation.

Huh? Since when does The Old Man buy me birthday presents?

He always remembers my birthday. Each year I receive a telegram from the Cold War outpost and when we visit, I'm always handed a folded birthday note: a fiver, since passing the eleven-plus, though when I was younger it'd be a ten-bob note or a pound.

Opening the little black velvet box, I see a ring nestling inside the white satin surround. It's gold with an intricate curly mounting either side of quite a big pale yellow stone.

Jewellery has yet to hold much interest for me, though Molly has one very pretty pearl choker with a diamante clasp, which fascinates me. Yet when I try the ring on, it seems heavy and incongruous. I can't imagine wearing it. It's a grown-up ring, sure. But it just doesn't look right on my hand.

'Looks like a topaz or a citrine,' Molly tells me later, when I go into the kitchen to show it to her. She too is a bit bemused by The Old Man's offering, considering my birthday is a few weeks away.

'I don't know why he did that, Jac. Maybe he got it from one of his punters. You'd better ring and say thank you.'

The following evening when I ring BIShopsgate 5000 and Miriam picks up the phone. 'Jack's gone out,' she snaps.

Not wishing to get involved in the usual tirade about The Old Man's bad habits, I mumble my thanks for the ring.

'Yeah, I'll tell 'im,' my sweet cuddly granny rasps.

Then, in customary polite mode, she slams the phone down abruptly.

Duty done, I take the ring to school and show it to Larraine. She likes jewellery and has acquired one or two small but treasured pieces of inexpensive gold, given to her by her grandparents. She too wonders why he hasn't given me the ring at the appropriate time.

'Its not your birthday yet, is it? Wonder why he's given it to you now?'

I will never know. That weekend, my mum informs me that there'll be no visit to the East End to see my grandparents.

'Your dad says they're both in a terrible mood, been rowing all week.'

Only then do I remember something I'd half forgotten. Not long after Barb married Ginger No. 2, we'd heard the story about the big 'diamond' engagement ring The Old Man had procured for her 'at a good price' from one of his contacts in the Lane.

The ring, Barb later discovered, was worthless, a paste fake. The furious young bride hadn't dared mention this to The Old Man – but everyone else in the family, including her husband, knew all about it.

'Well I've thanked him for the ring, Mum,' I told her. 'But maybe it's like Barb's ring – a bit of glass.'

So young, so cynical. As innocent as I was around boys, my view of my dad's milieu was streetwise. Molly didn't disagree with me. She just didn't want me making things worse.

'Please don't say anything to your dad, Jac. The Old Man means well, you know that.'

I did know that. I also knew from past conversations with Molly that Jack had always been generous to his wife when

181

it came to jewellery: Miriam owned expensive diamond and sapphire earrings, a big diamond brooch, a diamond-encrusted cocktail watch and other good quality items of jewellery. Her wardrobe also contained fur coats, another symbol of bookie pride back then.

I just leave the little black box in the bottom drawer of my melamine dressing table and forget all about it. Yet a few weeks later, just a couple of days before my birthday, when term ends for the year, I get in from school to find my mum on the phone.

'Okay Ginge,' I hear her say. 'Yes. See you when you get home.'

Her voice is unnaturally quiet. She sounds sad. Something's up.

But I'm not at all prepared for the news.

'The Old Man's in hospital, Jac. They think he's had a stroke.'

My seventy-two-year-old grandfather had collapsed at home. He'd been rushed to St. Bartholomew's Hospital and it was a very bad stroke, a hopeless case. The following day an ambulance took him to an old people's home in south London. He died within twenty-four hours. Oddly enough, on my birthday.

I hardly saw my dad during this time; I was asleep when he came home and he was out the door early each day after that. Molly was on the phone a lot to his family but a strange sort of hush descended on our home, a kind of embarrassed silence. Jewish tradition dictated that he was buried quickly and neither I nor my mum went to the funeral, which was held in faraway Streatham. Then my dad's brother Nev (Ginger No. 2), helped a distraught Miriam pack up and she moved to live with him and Barb in the 'burbs. The Cold War has ended. In just a few years' time my grandparents' beloved North Flats will fall prey to the wrecking ball.

I kept that ring. At one stage, I wore it often, but I never had it valued, so never discovered whether it was citrine or topaz. Or fake. Despite my cynicism about my dad's bookieworld, I understood, even then, that my grandfather loved his grandchildren, though his relationship with my dad remains an enigma to me even now.

Some said Ginger was 'favourite son' and that The Old Man took pride in his eldest. My mum, however, believed her spouse got a raw deal, Miriam permanently abusive to my dad and Jack always insisted that Ginger alone follow his path, always be by his side, his permanent drinking partner, a very controlling influence over my dad.

Yet within our history, Jack's generosity had made the difference for Molly and me when my dad was in India: it was Jack alone, with his contacts and sway, who'd pulled important strings, handed over cash, found us a roof over our heads at a time, immediately after the war, when thousands in London were homeless and the city in ruins.

And my dad? He was utterly shattered by his father's death. Crushed. We never discussed it openly – we were far too embarrassed to even approach the topic then, anyway – and selfish teen that I was, immersed in my loathing for his drinking and possessive ways, I didn't have any clear understanding of what this all meant to us. From that point on, he only ever described The Old Man as 'My Poor Father.' And it goes without saying that his drinking, in the months after Jack died, intensified. Night after night he'd come home late – and blotto.

In fact, losing my grandfather marked a sea change in all our lives. Though all I could focus on at the time was, for me, the upside of it all: no more dutiful treks to the Lane and North Flats. For Ginger, the business of being an East End bookie remained as it was. He'd still be travelling to Harrow Place each day, diving into the George and Dragon whenever it was open, glad-handing the punters every night, keeping up his front. A self-employed man in his mid-forties with a wife and kid to support, earning a good living. But underneath it all, irrespective of all the double scotches and off-colour jokes, he was grieving, utterly lost without his dad's formidable presence, floundering in a sea of insecurity, whose origins lay deep within an abusive childhood. As we say now, he was an emotional mess...

My teenage emotions were messy, too, longing for an adult freedom but still having to handle the confines of childhood and a school regime I'd rapidly rejected. The truly unlucky one in all this was, of course, my mum, stuck twixt me and my dad, trying to cope with the upheavals of my temper tantrums when I'd lash out in frustration if I was awake when he'd arrive home drunk, yelling at him how much I hated our home, hated my dad, hated his boozy ways.

It was a desperately cruel situation for a woman whose instinct was only to love and nurture the child who had turned into Teenage Monster, a self-centred little brat for whom she'd had such high hopes but who now seemed determined to wreck her dreams.

I still feel only shame, even now, at my teen behaviour. In angry rages, I would not just slam doors to vent my frustration. I smashed things, whatever came to hand. A china ornament. A small clock. My fury knew no bounds.

Tears and tantrums at home, the sum total of my emotional state in my last year in formal education. In class I'd be handed detention after detention from our teachers.

It made no difference. Wild of hair – my mop was now unruly and as untameable as my mood – and sarcastic of tongue, the teachers had long given up on me. I was a hopeless case.

Yet there was the other, lighter side to all this, of course – the pubescent child's development into womanly ways, the watchful eye of the girl looking out for a fanciable or desirable boy.

After school, Larraine and I would sometimes change out of our school gear in a ladies' loo on the Hill. Then we'd wander around, checking out the boys who frequently hung around the school. Or we'd get the bus to Mare Street and browse around the shops. Our funds were limited but that didn't stop us from looking and wanting. We wore short Orlon cardigans (worn back to front) or short- or long-sleeved blouses tucked into longish straight skirts, along with plastic pop-it circular beads as necklaces. (Long strings of Pop-it beads were hugely popular because they were really cheap and you could pull them apart to turn them into bracelets or necklaces.) No handbags as such: just circular wicker baskets that you could hook over your arm.

As for the local boys, by then we were known well enough at the Hill club to exchange greetings with some of them, chat briefly. Yet we had also become acutely conscious of another, quite different group of boys hanging around the Hill and the amusement arcade.

These boys didn't venture into the club; it wasn't cool enough for these outwardly sophisticated, sharp young dressers in their early Mod gear, hand-made suits and winkle-picker shoes from Stan's of Battersea.

They'd nod hi to us – underneath their cool demeanour, they were avidly checking out the talent, too – but we also knew, through the club/school grapevine, that these were Bad Boys by reputation, a few years older than us and already out in the world, not still at school.

Naturally, this made them much more desirable. Style obsessed, they wouldn't dream of wearing a badly-hand knitted jumper, and they were already aspiring to cool, stylish purchases including modern jazz albums (especially jazz legend's Miles Davis's seminal album of 1959, *Kind of Blue*), Italian Lambretta motor scooters, as well as seeking out foreign movies with subtitles.

Larraine developed a brief but compelling crush on roguish Vic, seventeen and super slick in an Italian three-button, narrow-trouser suit. Bad Boys wore made-to-measure suits from tailors like Bilgorri of Bishopsgate. (In a few years' time, Sixties icons like David Bailey would lead the way to a stream of well-known celebrity clients of the much loved 'Sonny' Bilgorri.)

I too acquired a fascination with one of this group: Stephen, a dark-haired, brown-eyed equally smart dresser. Very cute. A Living Doll, in fact, to use the title of the Cliff Richard hit song that year. Who said the somewhat naff song couldn't objectify men too?

Neither boy gave us much encouragement other than a nod and a smile hello. Until Vic unexpectedly stopped Larraine outside the amusement arcade one afternoon and offered her a ciggy.

Confused and flattered, she'd refused and he'd wandered off. But from tiny beginnings, teenage yearnings take hold…

By then, though, my friend had already been burned: badly. One spring evening she'd somewhat stupidly walked over the Downs with Handsome Malcolm. They'd had the briefest of snogs. Then treacherous Malcolm, aware that his mates had witnessed his walk with Larraine, realised his girlfriend might hear all about this act of infidelity. So he had let it be widely known that Larraine was a loose woman: she hadn't gone all the way, of course, but he reckoned she was a goer.

It was a brief but disastrous episode. The stories reached the school grapevine – then as effective as Twitter – and the girlfriend, sadly, was at Skinners', so my friend was unfairly pilloried for a short time. Hence her hesitation with Bad Boy smoothie Vic.

'I should've taken it, shouldn't I, Jac?' she'd ask me for the umpteenth time.

'Maybe, but you don't like smoking,' I'd argue.

I hadn't tried smoking but in the toilets downstairs at school, Larraine had boldly joined forces with a wild child in her class, Linda Ryan, and sampled a puff from Linda's pack of five Weights.

She'd hated it. But now she was endlessly replaying the in her mind. Say yes, light up and you'd risk your reputation;

news travelled with lightning speed around The Hill and had she done this and even walked briefly around the back of the amusement arcade with Vic (a popular seduction spot for the Bad Boys, aspiring to a hand job from a charver bird, as loose teen girls were known then), she'd have been a woman scorned even if nothing happened. Yet if you said no, the opportunity might never come again.

Mysteriously, Bad Boy Vic then vanished, no one knew where. There was a vague rumour he'd gone to live in the States (A few years later we heard another rumour that he'd wound up 'painting the Queen's house', a London euphemism in those days for going to prison for a minor fraud.) Even his disappearance didn't stop Larraine from endlessly talking/fantasising about him. When she fell, she fell hard.

'Why must I be a teenager in love?' crooned Dion & The Belmonts – and later, Marty Wilde and then Craig Douglas, the lyrics of the song hitting the pop charts again and again, since the words reached so deep inside the teen psyche.

We'd just mentally delete 'a teenager' and chant the words 'with Vic' or 'with Stephen' whenever we heard it.

At the club, Bad Jumper would still ask me to dance; he didn't give up. Another boy, Peter, also started taking an interest. He was very short, with straightish brown hair and deep brown eyes with long lashes. Quite handsome, really. But like Bad Jumper, he didn't match up to my wardrobe standards, sporting an ill-fitting lumpy tweedy jacket and baggy trousers with turn-ups. Yuk.

'I think there's something funny about him,' I told Larraine.

'He doesn't say much, just stares at you, and if it's a slow one he kinda grabs you hard.'

'But he's nice, Jack,' she said. 'Maybe he really likes you'.

I wasn't convinced. Both of us were still having far too many fantasies about the two well-shod Bad Boys, near but yet so far. We were hooked on unrequited love.

In the spring, a revolutionary new kind of car was launched, a little car which would symbolise the dawn of the Sixties and the sweeping cultural changes ahead: the Morris Mini Minor, commonly known as the Mini.

The miniskirt itself, of course, did not emerge until a couple of years later. But the small car, economical, easy to park and perfect for nipping around London, was priced at just £496 in 1959. Through decades of change and innovation, it would eventually emerge as the most iconic of all car brands. At the end of that year, history was made on Britain's roads when the first stretch of motorway – the M1 – opened.

But it wasn't just new cars or motorways to drive them on that were emerging during that final year of the Fifties.

We may not have been paying much attention, given our fixation with Bad Boys, but something very significant was now taking shape: a huge economic carrot was being dangled before our age group via an economy that was now swiftly growing – and a jobs market that was approaching full employment.

Factory, shops and office jobs galore. For everyone, especially youngsters. There were jobs for young girls, school leavers in particular, well-paid clerical or secretarial positions.

This office-job explosion had never happened before on this

scale: in the Thirties, women like my aunt Sarah had gone to secretarial college and gained the necessary skills for office work. (My mum had left school at fourteen and found shop work in her late teens.)

Then everything changed when war broke out in 1939 and young single women were obliged to 'do their bit' either in the Forces, in voluntary organisations or filling the millions of all-important factory or munitions jobs to support the Home Front.

In the months before war was declared, Sarah had found important and rewarding administrative work at Claydon House in Suffolk, where many teenagers from the Kindertransport (the rescue operation which took in thousands of young Jewish children from Nazi Germany in the months before war started) were housed. After that she intermittently found office work in Leeds and in London, though it was never easy to find work. As for Molly, as a married woman with a husband in the Forces, she continued to work in London's Oxford Street until the move to Leeds with her family towards the war's ending.

Now those tough times were just a memory. Twenty years on, a new generation of fifteen-year-olds could leave school and move quickly into this world of full employment: they'd live at home, hand over money to parents for their keep, but the wages on offer were now good enough to leave them with real disposable income, money to spend on the things that mattered most: clothes, records, movies – all of which were now being created and marketed to their tastes, not those of their elders. A breakthrough moment in history.

In August 1959 a report came out entitled 'The Teenage Consumer'. It revealed that young working men between the ages of fifteen and twenty-four were left with an average of £5 a week from their pay packet to spend exactly as they chose.

The average young woman of the same age had about £3 a week to spend: for the first time ever, women were outnumbering men in the office jobs market.

All this, the report claimed, was a brand-new working-class market which was spending most of its disposable cash on 'dressing up to impress others of a similar age', as well as buying records, soft drinks, footwear and cosmetics. It was an accelerating consumer world, totally unknown to our parents.

'Shorthand Typist wanted. Barbican area. £9 a week' was a typical classified ad in the *Hackney Gazette*, one of thousands of such ads to be found in its pages in the last years of the Fifties.

There were ads galore for factory jobs too. Hackney and the East End had many clothing factories, all now powering away again, supplying the ever-increasing wholesale and retail outlets in the new cheap-clothing boom. Indeed, Ginger's two brothers, Ginger No. 2 and George, set up a small East End clothing factory in 1947. Hard slog – yet by the end of the decade they were leading prosperous lives, buying their own homes, taking holidays abroad.

So that summer of 1959 was hugely eventful in several ways. For a start, it was exceptionally warm throughout, the best summer we'd ever known. When school broke up for the summer, Larraine and her family took their first-ever package holiday abroad: a week in Blankenberge, Belgium.

They went by train and ferry and Larraine returned bubbling with enthusiasm for the wonders of foreign travel.

'Big breakfasts and three course dinners every night, it was fantastic,' she reported. Even better, she told me, if you still felt peckish after all that, you could buy the most fantastic chips from a street vendor, complete with gooey mayonnaise or pickles – far superior to anything we'd ever sampled at home at the local chippy.

I was deeply envious. Probably because Jack was no longer around and things were bad between me and my dad, Molly and I didn't go anywhere that year. But the seed was sown: I HAD to go abroad. Goodbye Broadstairs.

I had my first kiss that summer, though the circumstances were less than romantic.

High on our list of social activity outside the club or the Hill was the 'evening in'. Essentially, someone would invite a bunch of people over to their home, which had been temporarily vacated for the night. The parents didn't have a clue that their living room would be turned into a darkened area where couples paired off to have a snogging session.

I cocked up big time. I knew my parents were heading off to a bash with my dad's punters one night. So, in the hope of getting Stephen into my clutches, I'd let it be known around the club/Hill that I'd be hosting one of these 'evenings in'.

What a mistake. Stephen did turn up for all of five seconds – and left. He could hardly have been impressed with the dirty stone stairs (thankfully no turds that night) and the smelly rubbish chute, though when I did eventually manage to get up close and personal enough with him, several months later, he was a huge disappointment: sloppy kisser with a personality that had been surgically removed.

As a few couples snogged furiously on my parents' moquette three-piece suite, Bad Jumper lured me out onto the balcony overlooking our street and, out of sheer curiosity, I fell into his embrace. We snogged for a few minutes – until my mum and dad turned up unexpectedly early.

Everyone swiftly ran off leaving me and Ginger to battle it out in a horrible screaming match. Now, of course, my father's very worst fears were confirmed, he'd seen it with his own eyes: I was en route to becoming a tart, along with Larraine and Larraine's mum who were both mysteriously the root cause of all this licentious behaviour. Molly could hardly defend me. It was all deeply embarrassing.

Yet when the shouting subsided and we all retreated into bed, strangely enough I didn't sob into my pillow. I still didn't want Bad Jumper, that's for sure. But importantly, like the first dance at the club, a hurdle had been overcome: I'd been kissed. Next?

These evening in affairs were hugely popular. You didn't turn up in pairs, you just hoped that the boy of your desire would turn up, drift over and lure you into his arms. They were relatively innocent. By then, we knew the unspoken boy/girl snogging rules: no heavy petting up top or down below. One undone bra and you were heading for Bad Girl territory.

Mysterious Barbara had told me on the bus one day that she ignored such rules – 'If I like him, I let him go where he wants' – but neither Larraine or I quite believed that, such was our innocence.

Until Larraine, together with another girl from Skinners', went to an evening in near Clapton and Larraine wandered into a bedroom to discover a couple embracing on the bed. The boy did indeed have his hand up the girl's skirt. Verboten. But it did happen.

She ran out in a panic. 'Oh God, he's got his hand up her skirt,' she told everyone somewhat thoughtlessly. It was a good way to get everyone's attention, including the settee snoggers. Like I said, this was still the era of 'don't say a word about sex or you'll be the bad one'. It took a while for her to live that one down too.

For all that, day after day of warm temperatures and bright sunshine has a way of casting a benign glow on everything. The No. 1 hit song from Jerry Keller that came out later that year, 'Here Comes Summer' (lyrics: school is out, oh happy days), had been penned to perfectly encapsulate the mood.

We fished out our swimsuits, popped one of our mum's towels into our wicker baskets and went in search of the perfect sunbathing and boy-spotting venue.

Springfield Park seemed a distinct possibility. But after one attempt, we gave up on that. No boys and not really a good place to be wearing a swimsuit since no one else lay on the grass wearing one. Next time we took the 38 bus and headed off to the Oasis in Shaftesbury Avenue, which boasted an outdoor pool. But we didn't like that. Too adult. No kids our own age there.

Finally, we opted for trying Larkswood, in faraway Chingford, Essex, one of the best known swimming pools in the area, with a huge outdoor area, the largest public pool in London. That summer was Larkswood's most successful – nearly 300,000 people used it. The beauty of Larkswood – aside from the long 35-minute bus ride on the 38 from Dalston – were the huge grassy slopes surrounding the pool. Lots of space for posing.

If I am envious of Larraine's holiday, I'm even more envious of her package-holiday suntan. She's one of those people who turns a glorious shade the minute she looks at the sun; in the posing-in-a swimsuit stakes, I can't compete with my friend.

Not only does she already look a toasty shade of brown, her swimsuit – a hand-me-down from her grandmother, who is a bit of a fashion plate –is gorgeous. A beautiful white bra top, very fitted, designed to show off a shapely bosom, atop a slenderising black suit with a halter neck. In it, my friend is a dead ringer for Gina Lollobrigida, a very popular Italian movie star of the Fifties and Sixties. And the boys certainly look, you cannot miss all the glances.

Whereas I, with a pale freckly skin and the same yellow and black elasticated number I'd worn since Broadstairs, look no more than what I am – a fourteen-year-old skinny Hackney schoolgirl, not a voluptuous dark-eyed movie star. Okay, I'm no Olive Oyl (a Disney character renowned for skinniness) now I own two bras. But surely, I reason to myself, if I could just get a bit of a tan, I'd have more chance of directing the eyeballing towards me?

The vast array of cosmetics and sun-care products now available to screen and protect the skin from the damage the sun's rays can cause barely existed back then in Britain's somewhat unpredictable, often rainy climate.

People weren't too aware of the damage the sun could do to

your skin, the risk of skin cancer, nor did most people trouble to slather on any form of sun protection if they went out in the sunshine. They just didn't think it was necessary. If they did get sunburnt, then they might use a product – when it was too late.

SPFs – the standard for measuring sunscreen effectiveness – didn't emerge until 1962 in a product called Piz Buin – a brand still around today.

... I'm lolling on my mum's bath towel, pondering the question of somehow getting a tan, when my eye alights on a girl not too far away from us. A lone female sunbather, she has just scooped up all her belongings and started to wander off down the grassy slope.

But she's left something behind. I'm close enough to see it's a little bottle.

Curious beyond belief, I leap to my feet and go over to pick up the bottle and examine the label.

It says 'olive oil'.

I have no idea what olive oil is or what it can do. I remember the awful-tasting cod liver oil from childhood: the authorities gave it free to pregnant women and mums of under-fives to help with kids' nutrition. But olive oil was something you'd only buy in a chemist then. It wasn't sold in grocery shops or widely used in Britain as a cooking oil or a salad dressing. Only sophisticated people who had travelled abroad might wish to use it that way – and then they'd have to track it down in an Italian delicatessen in the West End.

'Look! D'you think she left it because she used it to get a tan?' I ask Larraine excitedly.

'Mm... maybe,' my friend muses, though this topic is not her best subject since she will never need anything at all to help her tan beautifully.

Eureka! I can now get a tan and get more looks at Larkswood. With great enthusiasm I hurriedly, sloppily, slather the contents of the bottle all over my arms and legs. They're very white. I want GOLD and this is the way to do it...

It proves to be a memorable day, perhaps even more memorable than that first sloppy kiss from a boy I didn't much like. After a couple of hours toasting, we decide to go home. We'd already arranged that I would stay at Larraine's place that night: a ruse that enabled me to stay out later than my dad's curfew hour of 10pm.

On the bus, my face feels really hot.

'Does it look red?' I ask my friend.

'Yeah, it does. And your freckles are coming out.'

Freckles be damned. By the time we went to bed that night, I am in boiling furious agony, thanks to the bottle of olive oil which had literally helped fry my thin, pale skin. The Lobster Look. Bright red. Luckily, I've only dabbed a little bit onto my cheeks, but that was bad enough.

I am up all night, driving Larraine potty. We run into the kitchen and try ice cubes from the fridge on my arms and legs, cooling them briefly, but the burning is relentless. I toss and turn, hoping against hope it will magically stop and my torment end. By morning, my upper arms start to blister, where I'd rubbed most of the oil. My legs aren't as bad. And I'd lain in the sun on my back, so that isn't burnt.

Larraine's mum Fay finds some calamine lotion, pink stuff that forms a hard crust, which does help a bit.

By the time I get back home, I'm a very distressed, badly sunburnt teenager. Molly runs out and buys more supplies of calamine – and after the blistering and peeling in the days that followed, I learned a Very Big Lesson.

We didn't go to Larkswood again. I didn't dare go anywhere near the sun or don a swimsuit again for ages – until I spotted Piz Buin in a chemist and realised that here was good protection for pale, freckly skin.

Elvis still preoccupied us. We'd devour any news we got. That long hot summer he was on a very short break from his GI stint in Germany. He'd gone to Paris, had ventured quite close to us. Then we read he'd told a French reporter he'd like to meet Brigitte Bardot, which to us was quite mind boggling: Bardot, then, was France's biggest movie sensation and already making waves around the world for her pouty, tousle-haired beauty.

Larraine and I had gone to see her first big movie, *And God Created Woman*, curious to see what this woman dubbed 'the sex kitten' was like. Mostly, the film consisted of shots of Brigitte wiggling around or collapsing into the arms of ardent lovers. For us, the most interesting thing about it was the effect she had on the largely male audience.

'Did you see that bloke in front of us, moaning "Oh Brigitte... oh Brigitte",' Larraine giggled as we left the cinema.

'Yeah, he was in such a state, he was practically down on the floor, wasn't he?'

We didn't aspire to having quite the same effect on men, but Blonde Bardot was already a fashion icon for teens like us. She'd married actor Jacques Charrier that summer in a gorgeous pink gingham shirtwaister dress with a full skirt, so copycat gingham dresses were everywhere for the next couple of years. (It would be a pink gingham mail order dress that launched the enormously successful Biba brand in the mid-Sixties.)

Bardot's off-duty outfits were equally coveted: flat ballerina shoes, bouncy pony tail with dead straight fringe, slim tight toreador pants, all topped with a cropped top or T-shirt. Or full skirts cinched at her impossibly tiny waist with a wide black shiny belt. Simple but outrageously feminine.

Like James Dean's style, the Bardot 'look' started in the early 1950s and continues to be copied to this day: witness Kate Moss's much-envied street style. But of course, the other reason Bardot fascinated us was, quite simply, because she was French. That automatically meant stylish and chic. We didn't have any youthful home-grown fashion icons then, though this too would be changing in a few years' time.

At one point that summer, my friend and her parents had a serious talk. Larraine had made no secret of the fact that she was unhappy at Skinners' and her school reports – 'easily distracted', 'lacks concentration' – bore this out. (Mine were worse: 'frequently disruptive in class' was an oft-repeated one.)

That September, Larraine would turn fifteen. She could quit Skinners', get some commercial training at college and be working within a year in one of those £9-a-week shorthand typist jobs. Freedom. Money to spend on clothes. Foreign holidays.

'My dad says I should go to Pitman College. They teach you shorthand and typing and he says he'll pay for it,' my friend told me. Monty was now driving a black cab full-time and the family were now, like so many others, better off.

By then, there were any number of colleges around teaching business or commercial skills to the ever-growing numbers of kids eager to qualify for office work. Clark's College was one we'd all heard of, with branches all over the country and several in London. Yet Pitman College, in Southampton Row, Bloomsbury, was highly regarded as one of the best: 22 guineas a term. Four terms and you'd have passed your speed tests for shorthand and typing. Provided you worked at it.

Neither of us really thought too deeply about what this would mean: working and having our own money to spend was such a tempting prospect, we didn't stop to question the long-term implications of abandoning an excellent grammar-school education for an ordinary office job where you took dictation and typed up letters.

In different ways, we'd both been failing at school for ages. I was now pretty close to expulsion after a series of really bad detentions and 'pull your socks up or else' comments on my reports.

So on learning Larraine's plan, I told Molly this Pitman idea was what I wanted, too. I couldn't leave in September; my birthday was in December, a few months later than hers. It was yet another spoilt child's 'I wanna'. But Molly didn't demur. She'd talk to Ginge.

Then another huge row erupted at home. It was petty but at

the same time, to me, it symbolised everything I loathed about my dad's attitude.

One night, he came home relatively early, never good news because I always hoped to be sound asleep when he got in. From my room, I heard him talking to my mother, then I heard his tread out in the hallway, marching to the front door.

'Oh great, he's going out,' I thought.

No. He wasn't going anywhere. It was about 8pm, but Ginger wanted to lock up for the night. There was a huge bolt at the bottom of our front door and I heard him pull it across. Locking us all inside.

Something snapped inside me. Already claustrophobic, the idea of my dad locking us in while it was still daylight sent me into a frenzied fury. I burst out from my room, ran and unlocked the door.

Then I started screaming.

'YOU BASTARD! WHY ARE YOU LOCKING US IN! IT'S ONLY EIGHT O' CLOCK! I HATE YOU, WHY CAN'T YOU GO AWAY, LEAVE US ALONE!'

At that point I detested my dad so much, I wanted him to vanish from our lives for good. I don't know whether I hated his drinking or whether it was his possessive attitude that sent me ballistic. Probably a combination of both.

In return, he swore and screamed at me. Threats to whack me. Coarse language. We were both venting our respective frustrations on each other. I ran back into my room, picked up my purse and key and stumbled down the stairs. There was a coin box just across the road. Frantic, I dialled

Larraine's number and luckily, when I pushed Button 'A' she answered.

I recounted my story. She was somewhat bewildered.

'You mean he just... locked the door,' she said, not understanding my outrage at all.

'Yeah, he wants to keep us in – like... like in a PRISON,' I screamed.

'Well... you could come here if you wanted... '

I didn't go. Yes, it was a small thing and a total overreaction on my part, but the symbolism itself disturbed me no end. I calmed down, we chatted for a while and then I slunk back up the dirty stone stairs into my bedroom, emotionally exhausted.

That Saturday, I woke late to find myself alone in the flat. I wandered into the kitchen. My mum had left a blue airmail letter she was writing on top of the fridge. It was unsealed. She must have nearly finished it, but something must have made her leave it, hurry out. It was to her sister Sarah.

Sarah, I don't know what to do about Jacky. She's such a clever girl but now she hates school, doesn't do any homework: all she does is shout and scream at us.

We caught her kissing a boy one night and ever since then, Ginger's been going mad, trying to stop her from going out after school. Which makes it worse.

She says she hates Ginger – and me sometimes. I don't know what to do, she's always been a one for tantrums – she gets that from Ginge's family – but now it just gets worse all the time.

My mum had poured her heart out to her sister in sheer desperation. I couldn't quite fathom this. Why was she telling Sarah about the rows?

I didn't yet have the wisdom to appreciate their bond, to see that two sisters, close since babyhood, their closeness cemented by wartime troubles, would confide in each other, share their bad moments.

But who else could my mum confide in? She wouldn't have wanted Evelyn to hear all about the problems of living with a temperamental adolescent, that's for sure. Rita? Hardly. They never even wrote any more.

There's so much that only children don't understand or absorb when they're growing up. In a way, an only child will inevitably be drawn towards independence: with adult parents and no siblings, they are perceived to be 'adultised' right from the word go. Privacy is valued – and sharing, of course, isn't always easily accommodated. Okay, I revealed some of my thoughts about my dad to Larraine. But I didn't share everything with her. It didn't seem right to me to tell anyone everything.

Reading that letter signalled my mum's distress at where I was heading. But it didn't alter anything. I didn't vow to change my ways, stop upsetting my mum, try not to lose my rag, because I was blinded by my intense yearning for the freedom I couldn't have: what I already wanted was to get out NOW, away from my dad, away from this shabby, rundown street. An impossible dream.

Yet now there was hope. I'd go to Pitman's College, do the course and then go to work. I'd be out every day working, and even better, I'd have money to buy things, go out at night, every night if I wanted. Ginger could carry on, tryingto stop me, but once I had my own money, there wasn't much he could do, was there? And, of course, I could always rely on my mum to support me. No matter what I said or did.

I didn't fear further combat or more upset; I just saw my own way. My parents, both lost in their respective disappointments – with life (my dad) and with me (my mum) – could see no reason why Ginger shouldn't write a cheque for the 22 guineas (one guinea was £1 1s) per term to fund the Pitman enterprise. Three terms and I figured I'd be out. Who said you had to do four?

Miss Gray, the headmistress, made her case when Molly and Ginger sat in her little book-lined office, telling her they wanted me out of school. She pointed out that the good free education still on offer to me would offer me something more of long-term value.

Miss Grey was right. So were the politicians who had been so determined to forge a better deal, education-wise, for the post-war working-class kids, get them into university if possible. Yet for teens like me and Larraine, the times we were now living in worked directly against all that: thanks to the economic shift towards prosperity, consumerism was now taking all comers with it, as it is wont to do. The sheer thrill of spending our own money on what we wanted – mostly clothes – was irresistible. And anyway, the headmistress was talking to two people who didn't live for the future or plan ahead. We were a 'have it now' family.

So it was agreed: I'd go at year's end. Larraine didn't return for the autumn term; she'd been formally rubber stamped to leave.

Some of the bitchier girls in our year were quite mean about her departure: 'Well, she was a bit of a chatterbox' was one of the nicer comments. Only surly Barbara was supportive, shrugging, 'Lucky her. I've gotta stay on whether I like it or not.'

Along with her other close friend, Brenda, who lived near Larraine in Hackney and whose parents ran a sweetshop, we found ourselves defending her move on more than one occasion, especially once Larraine started phoning us with reports of Pitman's. It was all so very different, she said.

'Jac, they don't expect you to follow stupid rules, just go to every class on your timetable and work at it. Some of the shorthand and typing teachers are NUNS would you believe? There's boys here, too, learning shorthand!'

'Why would they do that?' I asked.

'Dunno. Only a few. They look posh with funny pudding-basin haircuts.'

Since we'd never met any posh boys, we had scant idea of how they should look or what their career options might be. In fact, a few of these male Pitman students were learning shorthand because they hoped to become journalists.

We were leaving school because we'd now become wholly immersed in teenage pursuits: boys, buying clothes – and image, a perennial teenage obsession.

We couldn't indulge in posing for selfies – ours was not a camera-owning world; the majority of people didn't even have a phone in their home. A few dads might own a camera for hobby purposes. But photos then were mainly for special occasions. In seaside resorts, photographers prowled the seafront all the time, making a living out of once-a-year holidaymakers – holiday or wedding shots were, for many, the only photos they owned.

Photos had been around since the early nineteenth century – but camera ownership, like everything else, didn't really take off until the Sixties. So while we weren't in control of our own images, it was the magazine images that were working on us: influencing how we looked, what we bought or wore, as they do now, really, except they're available online, all day, every day, 24/7.

Advertising in posh glossy magazines for women was far from new – but now the newest monthly magazines were starting to aim their readership at the young female shoppers like us.

Honey magazine, launched in the spring of 1960, was an influential response to this new youth market. Before its arrival, however, the publication my friend and I pored over was a glossy, French fashion magazine called *Elle*. By then, we knew enough French to be able to read some of the editorial and while you couldn't buy the clothes in it, or even the magazine in dingy Dalston – things were changing, but not that quickly – we'd discovered it, by chance, one day in a tube station's newsagents in Holborn.

It was expensive: as an import it cost 2/-. But in those early post-Skinners' times, it became a monthly bible. Shops like Printemps in the heart of Paris stocked the fashionable younger styles we lusted for: stripey swimsuits, giant leather handbags, tiny cotton T-shirts with a discreet anchor motif in the middle. Parisian chic at fairly affordable prices. If only we could get to Paris and buy some of these clothes...

Magazines are aspirational and this one worked for me, perhaps because it reflected a different culture. Cut-out images of the models in French *Elle* had started to appear on my wall by the time I was leaving Skinners'. They all had sleek, straight glossy dark or blonde hair, moody straight fringes: mine remained curly, shoulder length – and dirty brown. Distinctly unfashionable.

With freedom from school looming, I had to change all that. A new hair salon, Richard Graham, opened on the corner of Shacklewell Lane and Stoke Newington Road. Molly started going there for a regular perm to give her the curlier, shorter look beloved of most women in their forties. (Many opted for the 'Toni' home perm – 'Which twin has the Toni?' said the advertisement, since DIY home perms were all the rage in the Fifties). But home perms weren't my mum's style. Soon, she was going into the hairdressing salon every week.

Tiny hairdressing salons were now popping up all over the area – the once-weekly 'shampoo and set' was now becoming an important ritual locally, now people had more money to spend. Even though the torture the process involved back then was off-putting: it usually involved a lot of waiting around.

Making an appointment made little difference in these local salons: most times there'd be a good half-hour wait before a somewhat flustered overworked junior attempted to wash your hair in a tiny basin, with water that was either too hot or cold, usually drenching you in the process.

The salon reeked too of cheap hairspray and an ever-present pungent smell of the ammonia used in perming lotions.

Ammonia is a toxic substance – mostly now found in household cleaning products – and its use in hair products was eventually minimised. But of course there was no 'elf and safety involved in going to the hairdressers then.

Once you were lucky enough to get to the styling stage, an overworked stylist would hurriedly chop away, then furiously attack your barnet with pins or curlers until it was time for the Big Dryer – a row of huge hooded contraptions where women remained for ages, hairnetted and pinned, stuck under the hood, endlessly flicking the black hand-held switch back from cold to hot, both settings equally unsatisfactory. The long awaited comb-out was mostly a disappointment, usually a half-hearted version of the hairdo you wanted – and looked nothing like the models in the magazines.

For four and sixpence I'd had my one and only Richard Graham experience – the longer curly mop chopped off into a short style, neither a bob or a bubble cut à la Liz Taylor.

I hated it. I just looked… ordinary. No more pony tail, either.

There had to be a solution to my dilemma. Then I remembered. Some wag at school had tipped me off: you could easily transform yourself into a hottie, a real object of desire, by going blonde. On the cheap.

A purchase of a bottle of hydrogen peroxide from Boots on the High Street would do the trick…

CHAPTER 8

NEW WORLDS

I was not destined to become a Bardot-style teen babe. The bottle of peroxide, purchased for 1/6, proved a disastrous idea.

As usual, without understanding what I was doing, or discussing it with all and sundry, I'd dabbed some of the very smelly liquid onto cotton wool, grabbed some chunks of hair at the front and clumsily transferred the liquid to my hair.

Nothing happened. So I dabbed more on. Again and again.

The next morning brought a result: streaky orange, not blonde or even yellow. Unable to leave well alone, I continued to dab away until I'd acquired what was certainly a different look: I was now a short-haired carrot top. Orange hair. Nowadays you can have hair any colour you like: orange, purple, take your pick. No one even bats an eyelid. Not then.

Molly was horrified.

'What have you DONE to your lovely hair, Jac?' she cried.

'It's more grown up, Mum,' was my response, though I knew, deep down, I'd made a stupid mistake, just like the olive oil incident. That night, I tried washing it in the bathroom with a little ninepenny sachet of Sunsilk cream shampoo ('perfect for dry or difficult hair') to see if that helped. It didn't. Still orange.

The thing was, dyeing your hair was somewhat frowned upon then. There were products you could buy to lighten it up – like Hiltone, which coyly promised to keep it looking natural but 'perfectly fair' for the price of 5/10 – but a proper dye job implied 'woman of easy virtue', so if you boldly went from brown to blonde you were courting tart status.

Ginger said nothing: as far as he was concerned, I was already hitting the road to Tartdom.

Yet none of this 'don't do it' or my Big Mistake stalled my growing determination to be a blonde: within a few years, I'd opted for a salon dyeing job (not much better than the peroxide dabbing given the limitations of the products hairdressers used then and the real colour of my hair) and became 'Blonde Jacky'. Though in truth, once I'd acquired the stiff, bleached blonde hair I'd so craved, I did look a bit of a tart. One with damaged hair.

In my last months at school, two girls in my year became the focus of a great deal of gossip and rumour. We never heard a word from the teachers, but the abrupt, virtually overnight departure of Pamela Edwards, the sporty one of the fabulous swinging pony tail, created much speculation around the building.

One of her close friends eventually revealed that Pam had discovered she was pregnant. She hadn't tried subterfuge; she'd boldly gone and told the teachers exactly what was happening. She was going steady and her boyfriend, we heard, was quite a bit older than her, in his twenties. But even being the favourite star of the netball pitch didn't help with the teachers; she disappeared from school for good. A bit like what used to happen in the Second World War when they chalked the names of the pilots and their next bombing mission up on a big blackboard in the ops room. If a pilot 'bought it' (got killed) the supervisor would silently erase their name from the board. An ugly comparison perhaps, but just as stark.

The teachers couldn't stand the very idea of pregnancy. After I'd left, I heard that even one of their own – a young married woman – was ordered to wear a special concealing big white coat – to disguise her pregnancy from everyone else. What were they like?

It wasn't too long after Pamela's vanishing act that we were called into assembly for a special announcement. It was brief. But it was far more distressing than Pamela's story.

A girl in my year, but not in my class, a very pretty girl, Angela Mayhew, had died unexpectedly.

'She had a fatal accident at a railway station,' the head told us.

In fact, it was suicide. She had thrown herself in front of an incoming train at Hackney Downs station.

We filed out soberly. A huge shock for everyone. I knew her by sight, just to say hi to. Those that knew her well claimed that Angela, who had also been going steady for a year or more, practically engaged, had discovered she too was pregnant. Someone said she jumped because just couldn't face telling her parents.

Had these girls given in to pressure from their boyfriends to 'go all the way'? Or had they been passionately enthusiastic about losing their virginity, with a life ahead with their boyfriend already mapped out? No one would ever know. But their stories underline the fact that in 1959, the harsh attitudes to sex outside marriage or illegitimacy that had prevailed a century before had not yet changed very much.

Yet in the world beyond Skinners', overall attitudes to sex between consenting adults were starting to shift.

It was the cinema that initially started to reflect this to the wider world. Post-war movies had been subject to rigid censorship – a 1953 biker movie, *The Wild One*, starring Marlon Brando, was not shown in the UK until 1968 because the censor felt it showed 'a spectacle of unbridled hooliganism' (1953, of course, was the era of decent society's bête noire, the Teddy boy, and the authorities were hell bent on preventing any form of public disorder).

Yet one very successful British movie, *Room at the Top*, released in 1959, made a huge impact on audiences, mostly because of its very realistic portrayal of an intensely sexual love affair between a youthful on-the-make Northern lad, Joe Lampton (played by Laurence Harvey) and a much older married woman, Alice Aisgill (played to stunning effect by French actress Simone Signoret who won an Oscar for her performance the following year).

The story, based on a novel by author John Braine, was considered quite shocking at the time. Not only did it depict a very earthy ten-year age gap relationship between Joe and Alice, it also took a harsh look at the British class divide, where Joe, working class to the core, simultaneously wooed a beautiful wealthy teenager, Susan Brown (Heather Sears), whom he seduced and married – because she was 'in the pudding club' (pregnant).

This proved to be a landmark movie: the very first of a spate of British 'New Wave' movies with adult storylines and gritty realism that emerged in the next few years: *Saturday Night and Sunday Morning*, *A Taste of Honey*, *The L-Shaped Room* and *A Kind of Loving* all boldly tackled previously 'hidden' subjects like adultery, homosexuality, sex before marriage and illegitimacy on the screen.

As 1960 dawned, the curtain was going down on my secondary education. At home, Ginger was starting to become somewhat preoccupied with the future.

The word was, the authorities were about to change the laws around betting. A new Betting and Gaming Act would allow pubs to introduce slot machines and the world of the illegal bookie would end for ever with the introduction of legal betting shops. No more street or pub betting on the sly – betting was going legit.

This was big news. My dad would still be a bookie but he'd have the option of running his own betting shop at 11 Harrow Place. No more bungs to the coppers in the George. Adios to the elderly wheezy runners in long belted macs and flat caps, complete with fag glued to the lower lip, as they carried the bets twixt punter and Ginger in the pub.

The impact of this change didn't really sink in with me; I was too young to grasp the implications and anyway, he wouldn't be doing anything different. Yet there were lots of overheard conversations between my parents.

'I think I've found a good backer, Mol,' Ginger told my mum one night.

This was true. A man called Leslie, who lived in Clapton and had known my parents for years, agreed to bankroll the setting up of the new shop; effectively Leslie was taking over where Jack had left off when he died: the man with the cash backup. Molly later put me in the picture.

'It's good news, Jac, because Leslie has lots of other business interests so he'll just be there in the background. He won't interfere in any way. And he's a very nice man.'

Perhaps because of all this, maybe because his relationship with Miriam had never been good, Ginger no longer insisted I pay my respects to my grandmother, now living in far-away Essex with my Aunt Doris and her family.

For a while, Miriam had remained under Barb and Ginger No. 2's roof. But Miriam, with Jack gone, now had a somewhat different role: grieving widow, making life difficult for everyone around her. With no one to battle with any more, she just became more and more crotchety, demanding this, refusing that, behaving possessively until Barb, the memory of life with Miriam as a young bride still vivid, put her foot down. Again.

'She's got to go,' Barb told Ginger No. 2. 'Every time I say I'm going out of the house she wants to know how long I'm going out for.

'She's like my jailer.'

So my dad's sister Doris hosted her mother in her final years. Doris didn't say much about it all, she just quietly got on with it. We never heard how she coped with Miriam's demands. But then, I don't think my dad visited Miriam more than a couple of times in the years after his dad died.

Molly and I went once for tea. It was uncomfortable. Doris fussed around with cakes and sugary biscuits from Grodzinski in the usual way, Miriam looked exactly the same, pink-cheeked, white hair swept up in a big tortoiseshell comb. She didn't look thin or frail or even that ancient, just exactly the same as she had throughout my childhood. Yet she made no attempt at pleasantries.

'Now Jack's gone, I just wanna go too, Molly,' she moaned. 'I should've gone into that grave with 'im – but the boys stopped me.'

There was no answer to that. I briefly kissed her soft pink cheek as we left, somewhat relieved. Fifty years of marriage to a toy boy had not, it seemed, left her with any outward pride or comfort in her family, who were, after all, doing the best they could. To the last, only Jack seemed to matter.

Miriam was eighty-three when she died in hospital in 1963. Molly told me afterwards that when my dad dutifully walked into the ward to sit by her bedside, attempt a pleasant farewell, she showered him with a range of unprintable expletives. A tough-as-boots East Ender to the final breath.

As for me, leaving school was remarkably uneventful. Painless. The teachers were largely indifferent. I farewelled my cronies – the gang on the bus were all, except for Barbara, somewhat noncommittal about where I was heading in life – but then, their focus was fixed, with engagement-party venues already being discussed by their respective families.

Barbara and I agreed to keep in touch by phone. Yet oddly enough, this never happened. I never saw her again. Molly, hoping against hope that my new path at Pitman's might lead to peace in our time, said she'd buy me a new smart outfit, both to celebrate the end of my schooldays and my first day at Pitman College. Which was pretty generous, given the grief I'd been giving her.

'I've seen what I want, Mum, a two-piece from Lewis Separates,' I chirped.

I had only recently discovered the local Lewis Separates shop. It was part of a rapidly expanding chain of clothing shops (started by a man called Bernard Lewis on an East End bombsite), specialising in stylish skirts and tops for teens and twenty-somethings. The chain then morphed into the highly popular Chelsea Girl, a big retail success story of the Sixties, and over time became River Island, one of the UK's most high-profile high-street clothing chains.

My new outfit from Lewis Separates in Mare Street was a grey-and-white Prince of Wales check two-piece suit in a very fine wool mix fabric with a boxy jacket and a below-the-knee straight skirt topped with a pale yellow Orlon cardi. Combined with the Dolcis kitten heels and seamless stockings, it felt incredibly adult. Perhaps the strange red carrot-top didn't quite make the picture a match for the slinky model cut-outs on my wall. But you've got to start somewhere...

The Hill Club and a few Skinners' friends would still play a part in my life during my time as a Pitman student.

Yet Pitman's in Southampton Row, Holborn, did not, as I'd imagined, prove to be a mere halfway house, a staging post towards a working life. Going there daily, to an area bordering the West End, would lead to a permanent change in my social life too.

Travelling 'up West' to central London for entertainment or shopping was nothing new: it was something our parents did all their lives, given our proximity to the centre of London.

Yet by 1960, the West End was starting to change. It had always been the entertainment, shopping and dining focus for visitors to the capital. Now, as more businesses flourished, new offices set up and car ownership was starting to soar, parking meters were beginning to sprout up everywhere. (The first, in June 1958, was in Grosvenor Square, price 6/- for one hour.) By September 1960, London's first-ever traffic wardens made their bid for popularity on the city's streets (initial fines were £2).

As the tourist or visitor numbers started to climb in London for the first time since the Second World War had ended, different types of shops and eating or drinking places were also springing up – and the one place this was most in evidence was within the tiny narrow streets of Soho, traditionally London's most vibrant, lively melting pot, where various nationalities could congregate, eat, drink or while away their time in a vibrant, exciting atmosphere.

French, Chinese, Italian communities, long habitués of the area, had been making their distinctive impact on Soho's restaurant scene since the end of the war.

Yet it was the tiny Italian espresso and coffee bars, which had started to spring up since the Forties, that became the magnet to draw in the youngsters: here, teenagers drank coffee, listened to rock 'n' roll music on the juke box and took in all the excitement of hanging out in London's most louche of areas. Unlike the rest of the West End, some of these newer coffee bars stayed open both day and night. Which made them doubly appealing to students.

Soho, of course, was renowned as the city's red light district – but with the new arrivals of tourists, the authorities wanted to change this. By 1959, with the introduction of the Street Offences Act, an attempt to 'clean up' Soho by stricter controls of street prostitution made it illegal for a prostitute to wait for or solicit business in a street or public place.

Effectively, all this did was move the girls off the streets and into the buildings of the rabbit warren of Soho's streets, and clip joints and strip clubs began proliferate the area. The area's distinctive red phone boxes gradually became host to hundreds of hooker calling cards, stuck wherever there was a space: 'Yvonne, busty brunette, available all hours call MAYfair 2939'.

So by removing the girls from the streets, to the passing observer, at least, the area seemed relatively unthreatening. And by day, of course, Soho was uniquely glamorous, since Wardour Street, the thoroughfare running from Oxford Street down to Shaftesbury Avenue, hosted all the major film companies: you'd frequently spot fat-walleted producers with equally fat stomachs puffing big cigars or good-looking actors strolling around the area, usually on their way to expense-account lunches in places like Kettner's on Romilly Street (Oscar Wilde's former haunt) or L'Escargot on Greek Street.

In the earlier post-war years, it had tended to be the more Bohemian-type art students who frequented Soho's tiny coffee bars, paying 9d for a cup of coffee in places like Old Compton Street's Moka, 2i's or Heaven and Hell, or crowding into the traditional jazz clubs like Cy Laurie's in Ham Yard, Great Windmill Street or Ken Colyer's club in Frith Street. But by the time of the 'clean-up' a different type of youngster was discovering the Soho coffee bars – and their tiny basement dance clubs.

The new Soho youngsters were kids like us, some already working in offices, eager to find more excitement beyond the confines of home and office. Some came from the suburbs, a few from the East End, but there were also foreign students, here to learn English, or young hotel workers from abroad, newly arrived to work in London's fast-expanding catering trade. All this just half a mile away from Pitman's.

Pitman's College was housed in an impressively large Victorian red brick building, five storeys high. It had a brand-new cafeteria – a novelty after the horrible 'eat up or shut up' school meals – but the building did not boast a lift. So you often found yourself rushing up and down the stairs between classes, almost colliding with the other students also desperate to be on time, in order not to miss a second of classes where the much-vaunted business skills including shorthand, typing and book-keeping were being taught. The place positively hummed with energy and a kind of lively optimism that the commercial world would fulfil its promise and lead us wherever we hoped.

My daily curriculum included French classes, run by a very strict French teacher, Madam Robert. Yet unlike Skinners', where the overall discipline and the rules seemed to take precedence, here the teachers just taught – they took it for granted we'd follow. Much more grown-up. Classes were held without much preamble and every student had a busy schedule.

The supervisor, Mr Morgan, had a very distinctive big black patch over one eye – though no one even seemed to want to speculate as to why, because unlike school, the students at Pitman's didn't spend too much time on idle gossip. Perhaps we were too young to join in their conversations anyway: many seemed much older, though Larraine and I didn't share classes because she was already a few months ahead of me.

'I'm never gonna learn shorthand!' I wailed after my first two weeks as I clambered down the stairs to catch up with her by the entrance at the day's end. Initially, it seemed impossible to grasp. You did your best to do what you were told to, but it didn't make any sense at all.

'You will, you will, you'll see,' said my wise friend who had only recently picked it up herself. 'Takes a bit of time but you will get it, Jac.'

Given that we had two shorthand sessions each day and two daily sessions for typing too, it had to happen: the Pitman's regime was intent on drumming it all into you with all speed. No let-up.

It worked. After about eight weeks struggle, one day I started to understand what each seemingly impenetrable squiggle really meant: a phonetic representation of the English language.

Typing was also a problem for me at first. We were provided with noisy, clunky manual typewriters with inky, messy ribbons, complete with metal covers over the keys so we would learn to touch-type. Classes were noisy and initially somewhat bewildering. The nuns who took the typing classes kept telling us: 'Concentrate, concentrate. If you do, it will serve you for the rest of your life'.

It was good advice. As you learned you got faster, hoping to graduate with good speeds for taking down dictation (mostly for office correspondence) at a speed of eighty words a minute (for shorthand) as well as achieving thirty or forty-words-a-minute typing speeds. These were the skills the office employers were demanding, we were told.

Afterwards, of course, we would learn that bosses didn't always dictate that fast, anyway; they were not uniformly literate. Thanks to Skinners', our grammar was generally quite good, whereas the men – and they were always men – who dictated to us or gave us handwritten letters to type up often had poor spelling. Some were quite clueless about things like punctuation.

For us, the real difference between school and Pitman's was an acute awareness that our dads were paying for us to do this and that it was down to us and us alone to actually do the work, rather than snigger about the teachers, gossip about records and boys and forgo the thrill of homework.

As rebellious as I was against my home environment, just knowing that Pitman wasn't going to be for ever – with school, of course, the future always seemed to stretch interminably ahead – made in a way for a short-stretch deadline. Keep at it somehow, move at a fast pace and soon you'd be out. Earning. Your own money in a little brown envelope, handed to you each week, complete with a printed slip showing how much tax and National Insurance you had paid. Big incentive.

In those days too, it was relatively easy for a teenager to find a Saturday job, an introduction to the working world plus a little bit of cash to spend. Boys worked on paper rounds, helping out at a local butcher's or on an early-morning milk round. Girls usually tried to find jobs in shops.

Midway through my Pitman's time, through judicious, regular scanning of newspaper adverts, I spotted what I thought would be an ideal starting place: 'Saturday girl wanted for Dolcis, Oxford Street. Must be numerate'.

I should have twigged at the word 'numerate', but so keen was I on the idea of being in a shoe shop, surrounded by all the latest Italian leather pointed toe shoes, priced at £2 19s lld orr more, I didn't understand what this particular job entailed.

Dolcis, the shoe chain, had several stores in the West End: this branch was ideally placed on the corner of Stratford Place, Oxford Street close to Bond Street Underground station.

I had visions of swanning around the heavily carpeted shop floor, handing out shoes for customers to try on, standing there as they made their choice, giving them the benefit of my extensive fashion wisdom, then guiding them towards the till.

I turned up for the interview in a new green shirtwaister dress from Lewis Separates, to meet a fearsome, ugly-looking man in his forties, Mr Etheridge, the general manager. Without a word, he marched me into a little back room, his office, tucked far away from the big shop floor. He wore a dark, old-fashioned three-piece suit with a waistcoat and fob watch and he had thick black-framed glasses and a bristly moustache.

He reminded me of Gilbert Harding, the rude man from the panel game *What's My Line?* on the telly. (Harding died from a heart attack outside the BBC studios in Langham Place at the end of 1960.)

Mr Etheridge seemed really preoccupied and didn't care to interview me as such; he just asked me where I lived, where I was studying.

'Okay, you start at 9 a.m. sharp next Saturday. Ten shillings for the day.'

My first day at Dolcis proved to be my last.

Naturally, the job was nothing like I'd imagined. They weren't going to let a carrot-top fifteen-year-old with no working experience loose on their esteemed customers, were they? That morning, an unsmiling Etheridge – who scared me shitless – swiftly ushered me into another small but cluttered back office, a tiny room piled high with old shoeboxes, a row of filing cabinets and a little wooden desk.

I wouldn't be serving the customers. I'd be doing clerical work, mostly writing out tickets and checking numbers, ticking off codes on interminable lists of stock. Furious, on my lunch break I managed to find a nearby call box and ring Larraine.

'They don't want me serving customers! I have to sit in a dirty room writing out tickets!'

'What you gonna do?'

'Dunno. I'll have to stick it today. I want the ten bob.'

And that was it. Once paid, I never returned to the world of shoeboxes and scary Etheridge. Had I stuck it out, saved the ten bob each week, I'd have had enough for a really nice new outfit within a few months. Later, I met girls from other grammar schools who had left for college and spent two years working a Saturday job in a shoe shop. These girls saved every penny – all to be spent on separates, shoes and matching handbags. That was what most sensible kids did with their Saturday money, saved it to spend it.

But I hadn't absorbed any respect or regard for money. I wanted my own money. I knew I had to earn it. I'd inherited a work ethic from my dad, as much as I loathed him; since babyhood I'd understood that he went out each day, six days a week, to earn the money we lived on. Yet I wasn't prepared, at fifteeen, to do something I didn't like to get that money. Why should I? You could always find something else to try. Couldn't you?

Boy, was I lucky. This attitude would not hinder me one bit for the times I lived in, thanks to the full employment and the huge demand in London for young shorthand typists. No 'O' or 'A' levels under my belt, just typing speeds. Yet job after job after job would be mine. If I liked a job, I'd hang around, stick it for a year or so. If not, I'd quit on a whim, knowing all too well I'd get another quickly. Compared to the hurdles kids have to overcome now just to get a part-time job in a supermarket chain, it was a very carefree existence. Fear of unemployment didn't exist.

But there were other, more pressing concerns during that time of transition. By then, at the Hill club, I'd actually met a boy I liked: there was Andy, tall, blonde, witty and while not a slick-suited dresser, he made me laugh. He was both wise beyond his years and studious, already planning to go to university. We dated a few times: a Wimpy on Stamford Hill one afternoon, a Sunday afternoon trip to the movies and an 'evening in', during which I discovered he kissed beautifully – but was not a groper. You didn't have to keep pushing his hand away, top or bottom. But he left London to study in the Midlands sometime that summer while I was at college. I was a bit upset but far from heartbroken. I discovered, for the first time, that I bounced back quite quickly from the loss or disappearance of a fanciable boy. A couple of weeks later and I'd be fine.

Very soon, a fateful visit to the Hill Club would compel me to move on to pastures beyond the area. On the particular evening in question, I didn't go to the club with Larraine but with Carole, a very skinny blonde girl from Stoke Newington who had originally gone to Laura Place, but like me, had left at fifteen and was also at college.

Carole was a bit of a boy magnet: stick thin apart from a very generous bust, she usually wore a very tight striped cotton blouse with buttons all down the front which made her look even more busty – she was also a skilful jiver.

Perhaps if I'd been with Larraine that night, I might have refused when Peter, the short bloke with the lumpy tweed jacket I mentioned earlier, wandered over for a slow dance. But I figured that Carole wouldn't be leaving the dance floor at all – and vanity of vanities, I didn't want to be left there, wallflowerish, while my friend soaked up all the attention.

One slow one ended and, of course, on came another one, 'It's All In the Game', the Tommy Edwards hit of the previous year. 'Many a tear has to fall/ But it's all/ In the game', yet Peter didn't seem to be pushing his luck that night. He didn't try to grab me just that bit too close. Just smiled knowingly when the music finished. Could he buy me a Coke?

Instincts are funny. You really do have to educate yourself, learn how important it is to follow them. It takes practice and experience of life to understand instinct because it's far too easy to reject an inexplicable instant reaction to a situation or a person, brush it aside because there's no apparent or valid reason why you've reacted that way. So you push your instinct away and tell yourself you're being silly.

I remembered the conversation I'd had with Larraine about Peter – and her saying 'maybe he just likes you'. Maybe she was right and I should give him the benefit of the doubt. So I sipped the Coke and we chatted away about this and that: me going to Pitman, his dad saying he was going to buy him a new car – one of those new Minis.

When he asked if he could see me home, I thought fine. A lift home's okay. I'll get him to drop me off in Shacklewell Lane. By then, Carole had already come over to tell me she was being escorted home by a boy I'd never seen before.

By that time, I didn't encourage any boy to come anywhere near my home. Ginger would be rude beyond belief if a boy so much as rang me, so I'd already figured it was best to meet boys away from where I lived. Sadly, I'd recently had dreadful confirmation that this was my best plan of action following a nasty incident involving my dad.

It had started out innocently enough. Not long after Andy's departure, I'd gone out on a Sunday night date with Stan, a very quiet, good-looking boy also from the club. It was our first-ever date – our only date – to the movies and Ginger had been standing, fuming, on the corner of our street, in a fury because it was after 10pm and I was Out With A Boy Late At Night.

Angry, drunk and uncontrollable, he'd let rip in anger and slapped me across the face. Far more humiliated than hurt, I'd run back home as Stan did a swift runner up Shacklewell Lane. Another screaming match. Another night falling asleep vowing to myself that somehow, some day, I'd escape this place of hell and frustration. For good.

There was no lift home when Peter and I came out of the Hill club that night. He didn't have a car. Oh, no, he'd happily take me home on the bus. (Later I discovered that he lived in the opposite direction, in Clapton.)

'Oh, Shacklewell Lane, know it well,' he said at the bus stop. We'll get off near Arcola Street.'

This was correct. On alighting from the 649 trolley bus to get to my street, you had a choice: either get off opposite Princess May School and walk down Arcola Street or get off a bit further down the Kingsland Road, just before Shacklewell Lane.

I'd mostly use the Shacklewell Lane stop because it was a wider, brighter thoroughfare with bus stops either side and a little roundabout. Arcola Street, especially at night, was narrow and dark; there were a few dingy deserted factory facades but it felt sinister and dangerous, a place to avoid when darkness fell.

My thought, as we sat chatting on the bus, was to let Peter walk me down Arcola Street until the corner of my street, then I'd dash off. I knew he'd expect a kiss – a bit of necking – but typically, with all the confidence of ignorance, I figured I'd cross that bridge when it came to it. A quick snog wouldn't do any harm. Would it?

What happened was this: we got off the bus, crossed Arcola Street to the other side – which was feasible as my street was on that side – and surprise, surprise, there, to our right was the perfect place for a snog, far from prying eyes: tiny and deserted Miller's Terrace, a tucked away cul-de-sac.

I wasn't exactly shocked when he took my hand and drew me into the lonely terrace. By then, I'd snogged a few boys, knew more or less what was expected. Peter was better looking than Bad Jumper, and in my innocence, I thought I was in control. Huh? In a dark alleyway in Hackney with a boy I'd already sensed was a bit odd?

Peter kissed me with considerable force. Really heavy breathing. He came up briefly for air and then kissed me again, his arms now encircling me, his palms on the wall behind me. I was quite an eager snogger then, not really understanding what it all meant but happy to get stuck in. Then, with my back now against the wall of the alleyway, Peter started moaning.

'I love you, I love you,' he breathed, kissing me again, even more forcefully.

What was he on about? Love? Was he potty?

Then his hands left the wall and he began to fumble around below. Not with me. But with himself. Before I could figure this out, he'd undone his trousers – to expose his male-hood, his pride and joy, not just to dingy Miller's Terrace but to the whole wide world.

I screamed. And then, in a nanosecond, the girl who never did games or gym ran as she'd never ever run before in her entire life down Arcola Street, fleeing towards the safety of home, kitten heels in the dust. I didn't look back.

'If he chases me, I'll scream some more,' I thought.

But he didn't chase me. Who knows what he did there, alone, with his unbuttoned fly, in darkest Miller's Terrace?

I realised, afterwards, that he'd probably planned it all, the mention of the Mini to let me think he had a car, the suggestion to alight at Arcola Street. But he didn't plot to get me into Miller's Terrace just because he hoped for a mere necking session or a grope. He was hungry for something else, something I was too young and inexperienced to quite understand. Okay, I'd heard about 'hand jobs' via the school/bus gossip networks. But the truth was, I didn't quite understand what they were. Even when I'd once asked Barbara if she'd engaged in a 'hand job' and she'd said yes, she had 'but only half', this merely sent Larraine and me into puzzled 'what on earth did she mean?' territory for ages.

I was a bit distressed afterwards, yet I didn't tell a soul about this incident. If we'd still been at school, I'd have probably consulted our lone guru on matters sexual – Barbara – but I wasn't about to ring her up to get her cynical take on what it meant.

The funny thing was, though I never mentioned the incident

to Larraine, not long after she'd left Pitman's and started work, she too experienced something similar. The story all came out one Saturday when I went over, as usual, to stay overnight at her flat.

It turned out that on the previous weekend she'd been on a bus, on her own, going to visit an aunt. The bus was almost empty.

'I was just sitting there, staring out of the window, when a bloke came and plonked himself down next to me. Then I felt an elbow, digging me in the ribs. When I turned to look, there was this young bloke with his hand underneath his mac, playing with himself.'

'So what did you do?' I said, not quite believing that she too had fallen prey to this behaviour. 'Did you scream?'

'No, I just jumped up and said, "EXCUSE ME PLEASE" and went to sit on the long seats by the conductor.'

'But weren't you scared he'd come after you?' I wondered, my overactive imagination already powering away.

'Well... no. I didn't think of that. I was too scared to say anything to the conductor. S'pose I should've.'

And that, I guess, was how we learned about men who have an uncontrollable urge to expose themselves – 'flashers' – men who would opt to use public places, especially tube trains or buses, to reveal their all or even attempt to masturbate in front of young girls or women. Cinemas were popular places for flashers, too, so we learned later.

Even then, I stayed mute about my encounter with Peter. Perhaps because he wasn't a complete stranger, was part of what we'd figured was the nice, safe, respectable world of Stamford

Hill, I kept it all to myself. As it turned out, we never went to the social club on Stamford Hill again. Simultaneously, we'd both lost our enthusiasm for the place. We were now so keen to be part of the grown-up world that the links with our less-than-successful school years on the Hill were all too easy to relinquish.

Elvis, of course, still held sway, though our days of cutting-out scrapbook photos from *Photoplay* or *Picturegoer* were on the wane. Out of the US Army in March that year, he'd even stopped over, briefly, in Prestwick, Scotland on his way back home, the closest he ever came to us – or so we believed. (There would be stories, many years later, saying that he'd had a whistle-stop forty-eight-hour tour of London in 1958, accompanied by Cockney singer Tommy Steele, but where was the proof?)

The news that he'd found a steady girlfriend, Priscilla Beaulieu, and the photos in *Life* magazine of Priscilla waving him off as he left Germany made it obvious that the pretty, dark-haired teenager might have been a serious contender for his heart. Even if she was just fourteen and younger than us. But by the time he'd returned home, there were so many conflicting stories appearing about Elvis and girls, it all got far too confusing. You couldn't really keep up.

Sadly, his new movie, *GI Blues*, was a let-down when it came out – okay, he smiled a lot, so you got those flashing white teeth and those stunning cheekbones but there wasn't much else to like (the critics panned it, too). Yet by the end of 1960 we were rewarded with the fabulous 'It's Now or Never', Elvis's biggest international hit single. It sounds as good now as it did then. Ditto for the follow-up 'Are You Lonesome Tonight?'

After a month or so at Pitman's Larraine and I abandoned the busy, noisy canteen and started using a nearby café at lunchtime. Our pocket money covered it and if we ran out of cash, neither of our households gave us much grief: I'd just ask my mum for a hand-out and Larraine's dad was pretty indulgent – though in her early working life, she did develop a nasty habit of raiding her younger sister's piggy bank if she'd blown all her wages before Friday. The Southampton Row café, The Green Parrot, served up two course lunches for 2/9: a so-called curried chicken with rice and chips followed by a fruit pie with watery custard.

'I reckon this chicken is rabbit,' I told Larraine, much to her horror, as I cheerfully demolished it.

'How d'you know?'

'Well it's definitely not meat or chicken. So what else can it be?'

Those cheapo lunches in the Italian-run cafés dotted around central London were great for the small pocket, though you'd never care to dig too deep into their provenance. Or their nutritional value. Later, I found one in Poland Street, Soho, just round the corner from the old Academy cinema, the art-movie house which once stood on Oxford Street. A three-course lunch deal for less than three bob, a 'brown Windsor' tinned soup, a rissole (made out of who knew what?) with chips and peas, all smothered in a dark salty gravy and the ubiquitous pie with custard. It became a regular haunt for years.

We had time to spare after we'd finished classes, so it was easy to jump back on a passing 38 bus, our conveyance from Dalston, or clamber aboard a 22 and take the short ride down to Shaftesbury Avenue and Soho in the late afternoon.

We'd heard about the Soho coffee bars, the 2i's and the next door Heaven and Hell. Everyone knew about them because the 2i's, in particular, was so famous for 'discovering' all those singers. Yet we didn't fancy them much when we peered in on our first afternoon foray to Soho, perhaps because they were, by then, very popular live-music venues and only really started to get going at night.

Nor did we like the look of the horror-themed Le Macabre in Meard Street (black walls, skeletons hanging, coffins as tables, skulls as ashtrays, weird sounds on the jukebox). But this time we trotted in, ordered our Cokes and just... sat there. It was a bit like our first time at the Hill Club – minus the spotty youths eyeing us up. Maybe we'd picked a flat afternoon – there were very few customers – but anyway, the place gave us both the willies.

There were, of course, others, like the Freight Train in Berwick Street, opened by skiffle king Chas McDevitt, who'd had such a mega hit a few years before with Scottish singer Nancy Whiskey with the song of the same name.

Skiffle wasn't our thing at all – skifflers were too beatniky, scruffy – but still, there we were in Soho, taking it all in, hoping for fanciable boys. But the clientele were either far too old for us or there just didn't seem to be many younger boys around at that time of day.

Virtually every juke box in the coffee bars seemed to be playing that summer of 1960's big hit, The Shadows' twangy 'Apache', as we made our first foray round those tiny, buzzy streets. Soho was uniquely vibrant then: even a more in your face commercialism

– new tiny pop up eateries appearing overnight – can't wreck its fascination today, especially for the young. And of course, Soho is only a short walk down Shaftesbury Avenue to Piccadilly and Regent Street. Back then we found ourselves entering the fabulous world of the many big long-vanished Regent Street department stores: Swan & Edgar on Piccadilly Circus, Galeries Lafayette halfway down Regent Street, Dickins & Jones at the Oxford Street end – massive shopping emporiums with restaurants on the upper floors and super plush ladies' rooms where we'd eventually spend time after work, primping and teasing our hair, applying make-up, readying ourselves for the night ahead.

My favourite shop was Neatawear, a smallish chain that had started life in Maidenhead, Berkshire in 1948 and gradually expanded into the West End. Neatawear sold what were then called 'Continental' fashions, smart-casual suits, dresses, separates aimed at young people who wanted an up-to-the minute stylish look; it was one of the first post-war UK 'young' fashion stores to source brand-new style ideas and clothing trends from France and Italy. They even designed a distinctive logo: a very cute black-and-white plastic shopping bag to take the prized goods home in.

Every high-street shopper today knows Wallis as a major womenswear chain. Wallis, which had started life as a market stall in Islington's Chapel Street in the Twenties, was also way ahead of the times when they launched their 'Pick of Paris' couture collections in 1957.

Wallis buyers would go to the Paris collections – unheard of then for any UK clothing outlet –come back and copy, by memory, the most attractive styles – like the iconic collarless

Chanel suit in a bouclé fabric, complete with black contrasting trim – and sell them at office-girl prices. Wallis won my heart and most of my wages for much of my early working life – they were especially good at trendy looking coats.

One afternoon after Pitman's, on top of a 22 bus heading for Soho, we ran into a girl Larraine and I vaguely knew from Hackney. Doreen was older, about seventeen. She'd left school early to take a part-time job in a local shop.

This was her day off. Doreen was tiny, bird-like with very short dark curly hair (it might have been a Toni home perm because it was bordering on total frizz), and she had plastered far too much Outdoor Girl Secret Magic cream powder all over her face, so she looked quite odd. Her lips were bright red. (An overdose of Yardley Gay Crimson). Obviously a girl on a mission. Where was she going?

'Oooh, there's this coffee bar in Dean Street where they let you dance to records downstairs in the afternoon,' she told us. 'You only pay a shilling and that gets you a drink too.'

This sounded like what we wanted. So we joined Doreen (who vanished out of our lives for ages after this, only to emerge with a baby a couple of years later) and walked through to Dean Street.

The coffee bar was called Les Enfants Terribles at the Oxford Street end of Dean Street on the corner of Diadem Court. It was run by a woman called Betty and the customers weren't like the music mad crowds at the 2i's: they were good-looking, quite glamorous, dark-eyed, handsome young foreign boys, mostly French or Italian .

They dressed the way we liked, tight jumpers, narrow trousers, even belted trench coats, the modish Continental 'look' we'd picked up on from studying the pages of *Elle* magazine.

They didn't look at you and say nothing, like the inhibited English blokes. They'd just come over, start talking in fractured English. These guys wanted to chat girls up, practice their English, and like us they were in love with the buzz of Soho – and life in what was now becoming an exciting city, a place of freedom far away from home for those here to study, work in the big hotels or in the Soho restaurants.

The basement dance area was painted black. It had a tiny little bar just selling soft drinks and a record player behind the bar playing all the latest hits. Perfect.

Soon we discovered there were other similar coffee bars with basement dancing, the Bastille in Wardour Street or the little basement club called St Anne's near the church at the Shaftesbury Avenue end of Wardour Street. But it was Les Enfants, with its slickly dressed Italian boys on their afternoon break from hotel work, and the trendy looking French students with sleek haircuts, that became our regular haunt over the next year or two, when we started going there at night too. We remained loyal, in our hearts, to Elvis. But this was the point where his lustre began to fade away for us as we danced with the intriguing foreign boys to the Ray Charles's sounds of 'Georgia on My Mind' or 'Hit the Road Jack'. It was only natural that we fell for it all. We were ready to be drawn in by the real thing, not a picture on the wall.

The funny thing was, Doreen was not the only Hackney

girl like us, hankering for the excitement of the glam foreigners in Soho rather than the local Jewish lads we were more or less expected to stick to, end up with. Once working, we would form a little group, about six of us Hackney teens, all firmly dedicated to going up West on the bus and into the Soho basement dives. None of these girls had gone to our school. But we learned, very soon, that word had reached our former classmates who were somewhat shocked that we had ditched the Hill Club and our kosher roots for something exotic and unknown. Let's face it – Soho was the city's renowned red-light district, even if we chose to ignore its history.

Larraine bumped into a Skinners' girl one Saturday afternoon in Mare Street, a girl called Maureen who had been in her class. She was still at school.

'I hear you're going down Soho with all the foreign boys,' Maureen remonstrated.

'I've only got one word to say to you: "DON'T".' Then she marched off.

Forbidden territory. Living dangerously.

What could be more exciting?

CHAPTER 9

THE 38 BUS TO FREEDOM

Ginger's application for a betting shop went through in the autumn of 1960. It couldn't open until the following spring but once approved, it would be the first-ever legal betting shop in the City of London precinct, which is some sort of distinction, if you ignore the cash flow my dad had generated in Harrow Place throughout the illegal days of the 'bung' and the runner.

The Fifties were over, yet my dad's over-the-top, possessive behaviour didn't change. Once I started working, there were still occasional flare-ups, yet a kind of day-to-day routine of avoidance developed, which cut down on the conflicts and screaming matches.

From that time on, we saw little of each other. He was busily preoccupied with the new shop, I was preoccupied with the new vistas that were beginning to open up for me once my working life started.

I'd like to add that our immediate surrounds, Ridley, Dalston and Shacklewell Lane, were magically transformed by the start of the new decade, but this wasn't the case. Everything around us looked pretty much the same as it had since I'd been a child.

The only real difference was that people now had more money in their pocket to spend or buy big items on HP – and the local shops were doing their level best to entice everyone through the door. Lively, noisy, messy Ridley Road market and its stalls continued to thrive and the new Wimpy Bar facing the market did a roaring trade almost from the day its doors opened. Cooke's eel, pie and mash shop further down Kingsland Road continued to be a very popular local haunt with the big trays of slippery eels on display outside: 'Jelly Deals' as I called them, were a part of East End life for a long time; it was only in 1997 that the Kingsland Road shop finally closed its doors.

Dalston Junction was my escape hatch: en route to the West End in the evening, I'd meet Larraine or other friends from the area at the 38 bus stop at the Junction, behind which stood an ancient, rundown and largely ignored railway station which ran trains (on something called the North London Line) to Broad Street, very near Liverpool Street.

Today you find the gleaming new overground station there, dominating the Junction, though the railway authorities closed the useful Dalston–Broad Street rail link in the Eighties because no one ever used it.

If, for some reason, I wanted to go up West by Underground,

I'd head for the nearest tube at Liverpool Street by bus. Like the rest of the area then, Liverpool Street station was cavernous, grimy and partially bomb damaged. (The station and the area around it would eventually be reconstructed and modernised to incorporate a big office development, now known as Broadgate, by 1991.)

At Liverpool Street tube I'd fish around in my purse for the coppers, sixpenny pieces or shilling pieces to pop into the big sloping-front ticket machines on the concourse, each machine with an illuminated fare panel that corresponded with the destination.

At either end of the journey there were no automated gates, you just handed your ticket to an inspector. (Plans for a fully automated ticket system did not start to be drawn up until 1962.)

Tube journeys then were quite different in that if you travelled once the rush hour had ended, it was nowhere near as crowded and jam-packed as it is now. Rush hour then really was an hour or two since nine-to-five people in offices literally worked those hours. The long-hours' culture was a long way away.

Back then on the buses you'd sometimes encounter cheerful or bossy clippies (female bus conductors) dispensing multi-coloured tickets off a wooden rack on the buses, a tad more congenial than today's lonely, oft-scowling drivers, struggling with the twin evils of traffic congestion and passengers who have no idea where they're heading. Once they'd boarded, passengers would usually offer their money to the conductor on the bus in return for the ticket, though the conductors seemed to have an uncanny knack of spotting any passenger who hadn't been so honest.

Sometimes we'd see women knitting furiously on the Central Line. On buses and tubes you'd frequently encounter a horrible pong of stale sweat emanating from clothing that had never seen a washtub, let alone a dry cleaners. Perhaps you can find that today sometimes, but as I've already noted, deodorant products back then were not widely used.

Fifties girls, including me, would deploy Cussons Linden Blossom talcum powder (2 bob for a tin) underarm as a means of keeping sweat at bay – or we'd sprinkle it all over ourselves after a bath, rather than smearing on body lotion. The talc smelled nice but, it turned out, it was not exactly healthy since talc in its natural form contains asbestos, though today's talcum powder, manufacturers say, is free of this. (There are claims that talcum powder can cause certain forms of cancer, though these are often disputed.)

The smell of ciggy smoke was also prevalent on public transport. The buses, including London's much loved iconic Routemaster double-decker bus, introduced in 1959 and finally withdrawn nearly half a century later, gave smokers free reign on the upper deck, so you'd encounter a terrible fug when you clambered upstairs.

Tube and overhead trains allowed smoking in designated carriages for many years. A permanent ban on all smoking on the entire London Underground network and premises was not enforced until 1987. In the case of London's buses, London Regional Transport made all buses smoke-free in 1991.

Yet with all that, a huge nostalgia prevails around those of us who remember using London's old transport network –

even around those odd-looking ancient Liverpool Street ticket machines.

It's easy to see why. Each one of those journeys made into the West End made up the days of our youth: the surroundings were irrelevant because for the young, it is the destination itself that matters most of all, the journey all heady anticipation of the night out, the freedom of the exciting opportunity to let rip.

In the end, neither Larraine nor I completed our Pitman's courses. We'd already acquired reasonably good speeds and that summer, a family friend asked Larraine if she fancied an opening that had come up where she worked. Jeanette was nineteen and, to us, in her stilettos and shiny homemade dresses, she seemed more experienced and sophisticated (she wasn't, she just talked a good game).

Jeanette worked at a small debt-collection agency just off Bond Street. They needed a junior shorthand typist. Within a matter of weeks my friend had quit Pitman's, had the interview and been hired. The pay was £7 a week with a promise of a rise if she did well. (It never came). She started work just before her sixteenth birthday.

'The boss is a Jewish atheist,' Larraine told me over the phone after her first week. He never stops saying "please God".'

Jeanette, it turned out, could only type with one finger of each hand.

'And she's always going on about what's on the telly. She only watches ITV, *Wagon Train*, *Emergency Ward Ten*, *Take Your Pick*, all of them. Her boyfriend never takes her out. They just sit at home watching rubbish on the telly.'

Cultural snobbery existed even then, even amongst teenage wannabe shorthand typists from Hackney.

As it was, we rarely sat down to watch TV, preferring our books, magazines, West End window shopping and the glowing attractions of Alain Delon or Jean-Paul Belmondo lookalikes in the Soho basement dives.

I was a bit puzzled that Larraine had been so quick to accept the offer, though I didn't voice my thoughts. I thought she could have easily got more money somewhere else: all the newspaper ads boasted bigger salaries for junior shorthand typists, some even promised £9 a week. The employment agency adverts also promised more.

As usual, it wasn't long before I followed my friend's lead. Pitman's took my early resignation gracefully and I was even handed the all-important certificates saying I could type at thirty words a minute and write Pitman shorthand at twice that speed. Molly and Ginger didn't question my desire to start working before completion of the course. My mum believed I was so clever, another month or two didn't matter. Ginger merely saw the practicalities.

'Won't be a waste of money, that course,' said Ginger sagely when he heard the news. 'They're crying out for kids in offices in the City.'

But I had no interest in the City or anything nudging his East End world. Only a job in the centre of the West End, near Soho, Oxford Street and all the shops would do. I'd get it from one of the new employment agencies. Alfred Marks, Conduit Bureau, Brook Street, Reed, all advertising daily in the *Evening*

Standard because there were so many jobs to fill. And there were plenty of other, smaller agencies springing up everywhere: business was booming.

In the end, I plumped to register with a biggie: Brook Street Bureau, launched in Mayfair in 1946 by a woman called Margery Hurst. Brook Street was a highly successful enterprise well on its way to becoming the largest secretarial recruitment agency in the country.

It was a sensible choice. They were a bit snooty – well, the office was in Mayfair – and I found, despite my beliefs, that without any experience I was unable to top Larraine's £7 a week for a junior shorthand typist, though her employers weren't willing to fork out for the 10 bob's worth of Luncheon Vouchers my new job offered (a scheme brought in as a tax-free inducement to ensure that workers in the post-rationing era would get a decent meal each day).

I'd be working for an American oil company in Savile Row, a street normally associated with bespoke gentlemen's tailoring, though it would achieve enduring fame at the end of the Sixties when the Beatles set up their Apple HQ at no. 3 Savile Row (they gave their last ever concert together on the roof of Apple in 1969). The job came with two weeks' paid holiday a year.

I had only just turned sixteen on the day I started work in Savile Row, knowing so little of life beyond the confines of home, somewhat nervous inside but outwardly bluffing, as usual, affecting a confidence I would never possess until a long time later.

I didn't have a clue about what working for an American oil

company might entail, nor did I put much thought into how I would deal with this unfamiliar adult office world.

In truth, it was all a case of location, location. This was where I wanted to be, just round the corner from my friend's office, a short walk to Regent Street and the shops and only ten minutes' walk from there to Soho and Les Enfants. My instinct was to position myself in the heart of London's West End: all the excitement, glamour and retail temptation a sixteen-year-old could wish for.

So there it was, my first step towards the freedom I craved, a daily escape from the streets of Dalston, a release from parental authority, a tug at the independence I was reaching out for, without really knowing why I craved it so much. Yet I could see, quite clearly, that any job at all would give me a measure of independence which would count for a great deal.

You could hardly say I was a mature sixteen-year-old. I'd ducked out of a good education, I didn't have any sense of responsibility to others that a youngster from a bigger family might have inherited. My parents never expected me to discipline myself financially, get used to the idea of handing over something from my wages, as other families often did. I still had a very cushy berth.

I hadn't learned how to cook beyond shoving fish fingers under the grill or even to do housework. I had not absorbed anything at all that might prove useful in domestic life. Yet to my parents, despite all the ding-dongs and fury, I remained precious, cherished. To me, my parents remained the people who might try to prevent me from doing whatever I wanted.

My mother, I knew, would always be on my side, though I was too self-centred to fully understand the good fortune I had in this respect. My dad, as I've already said, had become an adversary, partly due to his behaviour but also because he seemed to represent so much of what I wanted to flee from, though he too fully understood his own good fortune in having married my mum.

The ugly, cramped and somewhat depressing place where we lived was a permanent thorn in my side: in my heart, I was rebelling against this as much as my father's possessiveness. I wanted beauty, glamour and excitement. I won't say I passionately believed it was all there for the taking, but just wanting it was a great motivator.

'Disobedience is essential for survival,' the American writer Joe Queenan wrote recently.

That just about sums up my time as Teenage Monster, though of course I wasn't an out-and-out teen rebel as we might understand it today: I was still very much a child and children then were expected to play a far lesser role in the world than they do today.

It's quite incredible nowadays that girls at my school would find it shocking or unwise to visit a coffee bar in Soho and dance to records with 'foreigners'. Yet that small incident alone is telling. It indicates how restrictive and narrow-minded those times were, even if the stories about what happened to the girls in my year who fell pregnant had not demonstrated this in a much starker manner.

But if I was emotionally immature, underneath it all, I did

perceive that the world I was growing up in was rooted in inequality: no choice for my mum but to put up with my dad's drinking because we were totally dependent on him financially. So many women then found themselves in exactly that spot, at the mercy of their husband's behaviour, not just because of booze but for many other reasons. They didn't have anything remotely like the choices women have now. Too many lives lived in painful, unspoken desperation, far too much 'put up and shut up'.

The basic rituals of courtship, which I was only starting to understand, involved women waiting for men to choose them. This jarred with me straight away. Why did we have to wait? Why couldn't we be the ones to walk over and choose?

Of course, this ritual had evolved because a woman's key role in life was to wait on others, wife and mum, and you'd better be quick about getting there: in the late Fifties a young working-class girl's shelf life was short: unmarried and not even engaged at twenty-one propelled you straight into the tut-tut, what a shame realm of spinsterdom. And who wanted that?

Despite all that, I already understood that I would not be prepared to follow the conventional, widely accepted path of my gender or my background. There were far too many unanswered questions about it all for me to just accept it all, pay homage to the traditional role merely because everyone else did.

This is the point where my story of my teenage 1950s reaches an end.

But what happened afterwards, you might wonder? My earlier memoirs, *Bombsites & Lollipops* and *White Boots & Mini*

Skirts, give a perspective on the years from the 1940s to the mid-1970s. Yet it would be remiss not to give anyone reading this some sense of the years afterwards...

I grew out of Les Enfants and the afternoon trips to the basement bars in a few years, though foreign boys continued to hold huge appeal, and by the time I was nineteen I had discovered discos and sex (in that order) and gradually became embroiled in a series of love affairs.

My school friend, however, did meet her fate at Les Enfants. Larraine, eighteen, was swept off her feet by a handsome young Italian, Michael, who worked at the Savoy Hotel. They married, had four children, and Larraine and I remain good friends to this day. Sadly, Michael died in 1999.

A few of my other friends from Hackney met handsome boys from abroad in the Soho clubs and discos and married them: by the late 1960s, London was very gradually becoming something akin to the cultural melting pot it is today.

In the end, my escape from Hackney did not come until I moved into a shared flat in green and pleasant north-west London in the mid-1960s.

At the time, young women still went straight from home to husband; it was unusual for a young girl to move out to flat share unless she came from abroad or the provinces, but a combination of steady determination and guile helped me break free. I had to wait, but I carefully plotted my escape.

I shared various flats in central London and worked in many different types of jobs, accumulating a series of relationships, good and bad, with different men along the way, travelling as frequently as I could. Until an invitation from a friend materialised in the form of a chance to move to Australia in the mid-1970s.

I grabbed it. It made perfect sense, one of the best decisions possible for someone like me: permanently restless, the move offered true freedom and even the financial independence I sought.

I went there without any real ambition or definite idea about what I might find, but opportunity knocked and I grabbed it with both hands: within a few years I was writing fulltime for magazines like *Cosmopolitan* and *Rolling Stone*. I had an exciting and totally fulfilling career in journalism which had never been planned in any way: truly, I'd never quite dared to dream that such a career could be mine. But it was.

Still restless, after thirteen years in Sydney and a lot of globe-trotting, I made my way back to London. It was a very good time to be a magazine journalist – brand-new weekly women's magazines were opening at a rate of knots – and I worked as a weekly magazine editor for many years, then launched myself into life as a freelance writer and author.

My mum and dad watched, wondered, probably despaired many times, but in the end, there was pride in what the Teenage Monster had achieved, though my dad was gone by the time I really started to get into my stride as a journalist.

Perhaps I needed to get far away from my background in order to find my place in life. In many ways, I was a late developer. But that's probably true of quite a few of my generation: the post-war kids who were handed the opportunity to do all the things our parents or grandparents couldn't even dream of.

As for Ginger, his Sixties betting shop venture ended in total disaster. At first, when he opened it in 1961 amidst a fanfare of optimism, it seemed good news. But the combination of a relentless pub habit and the limitations of relying for business on a local clientele who could now wander off to another legal betting shop at will meant that within a couple of years, the little shop's takings were dropping fast. The 'big boys', the betting-shop chains, the Joe Corals of this world (now known as just 'Coral') made it much tougher for the lone operator.

So what did Ginger do? He started to gamble seriously on the gee-gees. Until then, he hadn't been anything like some of the dedicated hardcore gamblers that surrounded him. But through a fog of whisky and pub bonhomie, he figured he'd take his chances like the rest of his cronies. Big bets (I can't tell you how much because we never saw all this). But very soon they were big enough to cause serious cash-flow problems. If he won, he wouldn't cut his losses. Instead, he'd place another big bet. And so on.

His backer, Leslie the Nice Man, knew nothing of this; he rarely even came to the shop. In any event, my dad had another good source of cash: the friendly local bank manager he drank with in the George. Another overdraft? Sure, Ginger. Another drink? Make that one a double.

It's a sad tale because my dad, for all his bawdy Cockney ways, was no fool. He'd taken the easiest route after the war in joining up with his dad, but the times had changed and he'd been unable to plot any way forward.

Not long after I'd left home, the betting-shop venture crashed and burned, owing thousands of pounds to the bank. The business was signed over to my dad's partner. My parents were left virtually penniless.

Incredibly, the bank didn't chase him for the considerable debt. There was nothing to chase: no property, no insurance policies, no shares, no jewellery, nothing remotely resembling an asset that might help the lender recoup their loss. It's quite possible, of course, that the loans themselves had been handed out freely without too much authority from on high, personal relationships with bank managers then being quite different to today: seriously, what respectable lender would lend a once-illegal bookie big chunks of money? But at the age of fifty-one, Ginger was an unemployed bookie with a shaky future. Fortunately, my mum swiftly found a salesladies' job in Dalston Junction, which helped tide them over.

Ginger had book-keeping skills and the full-office employment of those days meant that a year after his crash, he found a permanent job for the first time ever. He worked as a clerk at the British Medical Association for over a decade until he was forced to retire through ill health. He died, after a stroke, in 1981. By that time I had already left to live in Australia. In the final years of his life, he had no choice other than to forgo the double scotches. Which gave him far too much time to reflect, ponder the past.

One day, not long before he died, he sat down and wrote me a letter. We had intermittently corresponded since I'd left, though he'd never mentioned his old life and our exchanges tended to be superficial, mostly postcards from me extolling the virtues of sunshine and wide-open spaces.

'How I wish I'd never been a drinker,' he wrote.

At the time, it didn't quite sink in.

But afterwards I realised how he'd been overtaken by terrible feelings of regret about his former way of life once he'd been forced to stop work.

Remorse is a cruel tormentor: at the end, he'd paid a heavy emotional price for his 'live for now' ways, though on balance, he'd enjoyed his nine-to-five time as a clerical worker at the British Medical Association, a wisecracking Cockney mascot amidst the somewhat conservative environment of that august institution.

There were difficult years for Molly after I'd left home, particularly after Ginger had been forced to retire and remained housebound. She'd relished returning to work after the collapse of the betting shop and even when Ginger found work, she continued working part-time as a saleslady for many years. She didn't actually stop working until her seventies.

In the late Sixties, she even went back to work in the West End, which she loved: selling bridal dresses in a store called Berketex and, at one point, fashionable clothing to celebs like Rod Stewart in a Regent Street store called Fifth Avenue. Attractive, outgoing and cheerful, she embodied the 'get on with it' spirit of her generation in the most positive way.

When Ginger died, her life took quite a different turn. She flew to Sydney and joined me there for several months holiday, then, not long after returning to London, she met a man of the same age with whom she would share many happy years: Willie

Epstein, a Holocaust survivor from Czechoslovakia who'd been in the army and arrived in England post-war. They didn't marry but wound up living in the same block of warden-assisted flats for over a decade.

I never learned the full story of what happened to Willie during the war because he too was a 'get on with it' person who lived each day to the full: we knew that he'd been forced to watch his parents as they were marched off to the gas chambers in Auschwitz, but it became obvious, as he got older, that he had coped with the very worst life can throw at anyone because he was an incredibly strong-minded individual who didn't flinch or give up easily. You could only admire his resilience, particularly in his final years when his health started to fail.

Willie died in 1999. Molly survived him by another ten years. She became increasingly frail as time went on and for the last eight years of her life she lived, happily, in a comfortable, pleasant residential care home in south-west London. She died there just days before her ninety-third birthday.

As I mentioned at the beginning, the other family member who carried with her, through her long life, the imprint of all our lives in those far-off days was my mother's sister, Sarah.

There are many reasons Sarah never forgot our past, not least of them the sisters' bond as siblings while growing up. But though I remained largely unaware of it as I grew up, Sarah had bonded with me too at the very beginning of my life.

It was her name, 'Sis', that had been my very first word when I stood up in my cot and delighted her and Molly ('Sis' was my mum's nickname for Sarah).

Even though Sarah, a war widow, moved to the other side of the world in 1948, the sisters' bond did not weaken. They had shared so much beyond childhood: the painful months of evacuation in Leeds at the war's end, as Sarah secretly dealt with sudden widowhood while they tried to help their mother, dying of cancer. The return to bombed-out London, struggling off the train with suitcases and a tiny bundle: me. Then sharing my mother's dismay at having to move into the cramped, damp 'temporary' rented flat in the bombed-damaged street I grew up in, Sarah keeping my mum company, then leaving us, carrying the secret burden of their father's story when she said farewell to him, before learning of his tragic end.

Those blue airmail letters, of course, were the sisters' only link: no FaceTime or Skype back then to link up loved ones from afar, nor could people phone each other easily from great distances. Yet Sarah, I only recently found out, had followed my path every step of the way.

She'd despaired when I'd morphed into Teenage Monster, but as I grew older, and the assisted-passage scheme of the Sixties started to lure increasing numbers of Brits towards Australia, she'd written to my mum extolling the wonders of Oz and hinting that I too might find a good life there.

Given the circumstances they'd faced in our flat before she left, and knowing how her sister's private distaste for the bleak, depressing surrounds of our home had been brushed aside somehow because Ginger had 'a good living' and we had everything we needed, it's understandable that she wanted me to get out.

Before I left home, Molly would sometimes show Sarah's letters to me or read them aloud. I doubt if my mum ever wanted me to leave and go to Australia – it must have been painful for her when I did – but my aunt was mighty concerned for my welfare in those years.

Yet my attitude back then was very different. To me, the very idea of even visiting Oz seemed daft: 'I'm not going there, are you MAD? It's BORING! There's nothing there but sand and insects!'

By that time, of course, I was in love with Spanish beaches and cheap package tours, Swinging London and being part of the mini-skirted, flick-up'd throng.

Yet Sarah never quite let up in her desire for my better life. In her mind's eye, so far away, all she could see was this dingy bombed-out street that her sister and now her niece were stuck in.

How wise she was. How right she was to quietly lobby for my escape. Even though her own life as a remarried woman in Australia had proved less than easy at first.

Her husband was a bossy man, an engineer who didn't expect his wife to work. This pained Sarah who'd loved her career in the Civil Service and had, after all, known a sophisticated European way of life until she her mid-thirties. And while she might not have envied my mum, stuck in darkest Hackney, initially she was stuck too, in the middle of nowhere, in a remote, arid country town in far north Queensland where her children Victor and Julia were born, until the family moved down to Brisbane and city life in 1958, nearly ten years after she'd first arrived.

A mum in later life, she'd poured many of her own dreams and aspirations into her offspring, encouraging them all the way to use education and learning to propel them forward. She succeeded brilliantly: both my cousins studied hard and achieved much in life.

So when I finally got myself to Australia, though Sarah was not outwardly emotional in any way – she was always a very polite and reserved woman – her joy in my taking that big step towards improving my own future must have meant much: we lived in different Australian cities but there were reunions and many get-togethers in the times that followed.

Remembering those far-off times when she would dutifully post those colourful Aussie magazines to us by sea mail, the postman dropping those little bundles of blue sky and canned yellow peaches onto our mat, when I eventually started writing for those very same magazines in Sydney, I'd post her the copies of my stories.

I knew she liked to read them, show them to friends. But until I discovered more about our family history, so much of it after she'd gone, I had no idea how much my progress in journalism had meant to my aunt, nor how very proud she'd been of the former Teenage Monster who'd once been the despair of the two sisters.

As I say, she was not a woman to show her feelings. Her generation were not encouraged to be frank, to cry openly or be vociferous or forthright in their opinions. Yet in her quiet, ladylike way, mostly from afar, she'd looked out for me throughout life as if I were her own.

Of course, the other key player in this story is the city of my teenage years, so much of it then ruined after war, our little corner perhaps not the grimmest or ugliest sight of all, but all of it a far cry from the London and the East End of today.

I went back recently. You always do. The factories that surrounded my street are now smart, trendy, high-priced apartments. No more timber yards or bombsites, of course, yet the old block we inhabited still stands.

It's been tarted up a bit: security door, trees planted outside, windows replaced, estate agents' photos of interiors with lovingly preserved Fifties features – even the tiled surrounds of the fireplaces look smart and inviting, trendy wooden floorboards, carefully sanded and polished.

I remained outside the block for a while, trying to bring back a sense of the emotional history of this place, the turmoil of those years, the rows, the yearnings of that painful adolescent process, the limbo world of the halfway house between childhood and adulthood.

Even long after I had relinquished my place there, traversed the globe, I had battled with the memory that this had been where I'd spent my formative years, the place the teenage me had been so ashamed of, a fragment of my past that would haunt me for a very long time.

Yet I could not retrieve any sense of those powerful emotions at all. At the time, they seemed to consume me so desperate was I to flee. But at some unknown point, through the long business of living, treading so many different paths, the past had been laid to rest.

In digging up the remnants of this history, I'd reached a state of understanding: I'd even forgiven myself for my self-centred fury, my dad for his battle with his own demons.

I had reacted badly, back then, against my environment because that was who I was, just another child of this resilient and strangely compelling historic city, growing up in a world that was just beginning to show it was not prepared to be tethered by its past.

Just like me.

$$172$$
$$86 \times 2$$

$$2 \overline{| 25'9 |} 3$$

$$2 \overline{| 12 \ 9 |}$$

$$64 \times 3$$
$$192$$